THE
PROCESS
OF
PROGRESSION

NAVIGATE THROUGH THE SEASONS
OF GROWTH WITH GRACE

ALYSSA EDLEY

WESTBOW
PRESS®
A DIVISION OF THOMAS NELSON
& ZONDERVAN

WestBow Press books may be ordered through booksellers or by contacting:

WestBow Press
A Division of Thomas Nelson & Zondervan
1663 Liberty Drive
Bloomington, IN 47403
www.westbowpress.com
1 (866) 928-1240

ISBN: 978-1-9736-7860-1 (sc)
ISBN: 978-1-9736-7859-5 (e)

Print information available on the last page.

WestBow Press rev. date: 12/20/2019

CONTENTS

INTRODUCTION

It never ceases to amaze me how many people are in similar situations as myself or have been there before. Aware but not sure how to bring about their purpose.

It is a struggle to go through life knowing there is a reason for your existence beyond simply existing but not knowing the "how" of it all. Like me, you will be relieved to know the how is less important when you know the who. If you know the who, you will be instructed on the how in His perfect timing. It may not seem perfect by our standards but it is right on time. This is why it becomes necessary to balance working toward your purpose (whatever you think it may be) and waiting for Him to reveal more of it.

During this working and waiting you discover how much of life is a test of maneuverability. How flexible you can be when life inserts a sharp turn or roadblock on your path. You have to slow down long enough to evaluate what lies ahead. Then decide how you are going to respond to the different processes of life. Some handle the curves and bumps more gracefully than others and ultimately the ability to handle life's curves, whether good or bad, is an accomplishment worth celebrating because you made it through. The true grace in your movement is seen through the growth you exude as a result of how you experience your experiences.

Growth is progression. It is your cultivation. A series

of your development over time. Although the process of tending to yourself is not always healthy or consistent from season to season, you learn to be gentler. Giving grace and embracing growth. Life should always stimulate growth.

Our life's purpose is a step by step process which was a struggle for me. I wanted to skip steps or bypass them altogether but by doing so I jeopardized the progress I had made. Skipping steps caused me to miss out on opportunities to grow. Stagnancy was not fun for me and it still causes me frustration when it shows up but it helps me recognize the importance of taking things slow.

I completely understand the desire to rush through the steps. Daily, I skip steps of a staircase just to get to the landing quicker (even if I'm winded by the time I get there). Quick gratification may be satisfying but it is only temporary. Although skipping the steps of a staircase can make for a good workout it is not the best approach for life's staircase. When we take life one step at a time we control the pace of each stride so not to exhaust precious effort and have to make a U-turn because we have missed our right turn.

Every step we take toward our purpose demands a different level of energy and we do not want to waste it. We put a heavy load on ourselves believing it will quicken the process but it hinders the process because it slows us down and wears us out. When we have overwhelmed, overworked, and overlooked ourselves we must pause, replenish, and restore what we have broken down so we can reach our destination.

And let us not grow weary while doing good,
for in due season we shall reap if we do not
lose heart. Galatians 6:9

If what we are doing is well intentioned, drawing us closer to the will of God, we will reap the benefits of our actions. We will be rewarded for the good we have done. However, the *if* is important because we can only reap if we are doing and not just doing but doing *well*. If we stop or quit, if we faint because we have taken on too much, it was all for nothing. We must start again.

The process requires diligence. It demands your careful and persistent work or effort.

It requires patient, steady moves to accomplish the task at hand. To take the next step. To advance to the next level. When we are working well (and even when we're not) He sees our efforts and will exceed them on a level far beyond our ability. But we must consistently put the effort in, in spite of the tears, the pain and the struggle. We can only do so much in our human ability which is why we have to activate our faith as a demonstration of our trust in Him. Once He sees our execution and faith come into alignment, He is able to show up and show out on our behalf.

The process of discovering our true purpose requires us to continually rely on Him. Full reliance grants full blessings. We get what we put in. If we half step we get half. Little faith grants little but big faith grants big. He can make things happen even with our little bit of faith, grain of a mustard seed faith (Matthew 17:20). Can you imagine what faith the size of an apple could do or faith the size of a watermelon? Woah. We serve a big God. We must allow Him to operate in His fullness. We also, must believe He can even when we, in our humanness, cannot. We may not trust the process or like the pace but He has phenomenal plans for us. It is He who makes the impossible possible.

Life's processes will be difficult but with Him there is purpose in the difficulty, the challenges, the pain. There is purpose. He is God, He knows our struggles. He also provides us with His sufficient grace. We, as human beings, in this world, forget we must not be of this world. Consumed by Him rather than the glitz and glamour. There are limitations in the world but there are no limitations in Him. He is an all-consuming, all-knowing, almighty God. He is, not us, which is why we cannot do it alone.

> …*"With men this is impossible, but with God all things are possible. Matthew 19:26*

The Bible, reminds us how essential His presence is to the process.

The pursuit of purpose is dependent on our management of the ups and downs. Our maneuverability *through* hardships, and adversity, not around it. Going through it is how we rise above it and reach higher elevation.

If you are at all familiar with flying, you may know (or

not) planes take off into the wind. The reasoning behind it has to do with the flow of the wind over the wing to provide lift and takeoff more quickly.

Life comes with the same opposition. Naysayers will come against you in attempt to contaminate your mind, but you have to use their tactics to your advantage and establish lift off. Letting whatever comes against you propel you to higher elevation. Higher altitudes await us. Prepare for lift off.

THE POWER IS
WITHIN YOU

1

VALUE YOURSELF

Value of life can only be understood by first understanding value of self.

You are valuable. A prized possession. Uniquely crafted by God. I can say this to you but it is not enough to hear it from me. It is nice to hear praise from others but you cannot rely on it for validation. Fortunately, there is only one who we should seek to receive approval from.

> *Be diligent to present yourself approved to God, a worker who does not need to be ashamed, rightly dividing the word of truth.*
> *2 Timothy 2:15*

You have to raise your awareness of who this is about in order to confidently work toward your divine design. Daily speak life over yourself and your purpose. Honor yourself enough to recognize the potential in you to move beyond the normalcy of your day to day tasks and fearlessly pursue the urgings of your spirit. This discovery will draw out the depths of your love and cause you to move in a practical pursuit of purpose.

Pep talks did not come naturally at first but overtime I recognized personal value if unseen is of no benefit to anyone. So, although uncomfortable at times I would speak to myself in full blown conversation as if having lunch with a friend. An opportunity to further explore who I was and who I wanted to become. The practical part tripped me up. Not the thought, idea, theory, conversation, but the action of doing. I had the belief and all the ideas my mind could imagine but turning my thoughts into reality proved to be a big challenge.

I could do a lot of other things with ease. Stellar

competitor, academic standout, organization enthusiast. However, not all aspects of my life were stellar, standout, or organized. I had to take time to grow to appreciate my strengths *and* weaknesses. Otherwise, I was too hard on myself and failed to embrace all of me.

To understand the true value of your being it is essential to recognize that before you were even thought of, God knew what purpose you would serve on this earth. Prior to your conception, He already knew you. God had already blessed you and predestined you to be an advocate for the kingdom.

> *"Before I formed you in the womb I knew*
> *you; Before you were born I sanctified you;*
> *I ordained you a prophet to the nations."*
> *Jeremiah 1:5*

God had a plan for you before you were brought into this world. ***He blessed you before He birthed you.*** You were purified in the womb because He knew the filth of the world would attempt to taint your authenticity. If you do not know who you are then other people surely will have a difficult time figuring it out but once you develop an awareness of yourself others will see it too. You will have a certain appeal. I am not sure about you but I tend to be attracted to individuals who are genuine and sincere in their actions. Individuals who embrace their being inspire me to do the same. In a world compromised by those who constantly mimic others God only wants you to reveal your intricate design.

The moment He chose you He became fully invested in you, as an individual, which is why it would be an advantage for you to be visible in your entirety. Transparent to the point where you can be seen clearly by yourself and others. Not to say you should expose every corner of your life because everything is not meant to be broadcasted to the world. However, shedding light into your experiences does tend to brighten the path for others so they may see a way where previously their vision had been obscured. Your enlightenment brings light into a place that may have once been dim. Introducing grace to a place once filled with disgrace. We cannot allow what we have been through to dull our shine but rather intensify it.

A common misconception is we have to be perfect to help someone else. Countless times it has entered into my mind in order to be helpful to others I need to get my life together. Before I can shed light into their situation I need to be sure all areas of my life are in order. As if I would be less respected otherwise. It is because we are flawed, because we have experienced similar experiences, we can relate to one another and be open about where we are. Right now. In this present time. Without feeling obligated to be anywhere else above where we currently are. This transparency is what allows us to see and respect one another based on the commonalities and variances of our experiences. By sharing how you maneuvered through it, I can now see an alternative route to get to my expected end.

> *For I know the thoughts that I think toward*
> *you, says the Lord, thoughts of peace and*
> *not of evil, to give you a future and a hope.*
> *Jeremiah 29:11*

I can now see peace where I once saw chaos. I can now anticipate the pleasant ending instead of questioning the trying journey. I can now appreciate how far I have come and get excited about where I can go. It is the renewing of my mind which allows me to bring faith, hope, and love into a difficult season.

> *And do not be conformed to this world,*
> *but be transformed by the renewing of your*
> *mind, that you may prove what is that good*
> *and acceptable and perfect will of God.*
> *Romans 12:2*

This renewal process acts as a rejuvenation of the mind. Refreshing what may have been battered or weighed down by the demands of one pressing season. Renewal allows you to move closer toward the Will of God. It serves as an indication of advancement and growth. I personally do not want to be the same person I was a year ago or even a month ago. I want to continue to better myself in efforts to better others. It serves as a compliment to have changed from one year to the next because the change is for the greater good. Over the year if I have not changed in some way I have not grown. I have missed the opportunity to increase knowledge, wisdom, and understanding. The opportunity to grow smarter, stronger, sharper, and more whole.

Your mind is renewed by what you feed it which is why it is critical to provide proper nourishment. Build your thoughts on goodness, righteousness, and holiness. If God is leaving it up to us to prove His good, acceptable, and perfect will, we better do Him some justice. We may need to prove it to ourselves first, but once we have understood His tender mercies and unfailing grace we must represent Him in the fullest. You may have never been a representative for anyone, at any point in your life but today take on the role of Jesus Rep. If you have acquired any wisdom thus far in your life you need to begin dispersing it. If we fail to reveal how we have overcome what we have overcome, we have done a disservice to His people. ***Consider the effects of what has affected you in order to have a life-altering impact on someone else.*** It is about changing the path of destructive, sinful living to one of righteousness. You may think based on your experiences you were dealt a bad hand and you may be justified in believing so. Yet, there is always a purpose. In your pain and in your triumph, there is a reason for every stage and age of your growth. If you adjust your focus you will begin to see the motivation behind it. What you go through is not just about you. Your way of handling it may be better or more effective but if it goes unshared your approach to a similar situation may never be recognized or utilized to help someone avoid a similar situation. I have to encourage you not to be discouraged if you do not get the same outcome or desired outcome as someone else. It could be, you needed to learn a lesson from this to challenge you in a different way than it challenged someone else because as similar as our struggles may be there are distinctions. What worked for you may not work for me because we are built uniquely. No one on earth is like you, even identical twins have differences. It could be a distinctive feature or personality trait but as different as we are, we can still experience like-situations. Nothing we go through is without purpose and being open about our experiences creates this reassurance. We can question why we went through what we went through and I am going to answer by saying, you cannot go if you do not grow. We all strive to reach new pinnacles, to do so, we must actively work to improve ourselves and our environment. It is the work you put into you that reaps the benefits of your efforts. ***Grow through life, do not simply go through life.*** To get here on this earth we had to go through something. We had to pass through a constricted, uncomfortable space in order to reach a new realm of opportunity.

If you do not maneuver through the tough stuff your potential for growth will be stunted. Think for a second, could what I am going through be a requirement by God in order to teach me a valuable lesson pertaining to my purpose. Any time you are overwhelmed by what you are going through, think about what God is attempting to teach you. When you stop to take inventory of your experiences you will see His present intentions. I see how His grace covered me in the midst of uncertainty. Uncertainty about the unknown, what's next, or which route to pursue. His grace granted peace in knowing He is present throughout the uncertainty. His mercy saved me from selfish decisions. Giving me freedom to choose but mercy to provide restoration or relief from a bad decision. Many times, God is trying to demonstrate the significance of the situation but if we are not yet keen to His voice we miss His instruction. I think we can all agree that we have missed His call from time to time but His grace for His children keeps Him calling. As He is our Creator, He already knew we would miss His call which is why He calls again and again until we recognize who is calling our name and we respond to our Heavenly Father.

> *Now the Lord came and stood and called as at other times, "Samuel! Samuel!" and Samuel answered, "Speak, for Your servant hears." 1 Samuel 3:10*

I recommend you replace Samuel's name with your own. We may not hear God in an audible tone but when we hear or feel the nudging on our spirit, all we need to say is speak Lord. I hear you. I may not have heard you the other times or known it was you who was speaking to me but now I know your voice, so speak to me. Teach me. Convey to me Your Will for my life. I want the purpose you have placed inside of me to manifest itself.

Allow me to connect with You on a level where I am able to perceive the possibilities and potentials You have for me.

1. Start by reading His word. The bible is a book of wisdom filled with knowledge to increase your understanding, broaden your perspective, and renew your mind (among many other things). Recognize His power as the source of your strength, then trust your ability to activate it. There are certain things He has gifted you and only you.

    Find it and once discovered, embrace it.

2. Be confident. He has done a good work in you. The world is not who has done the *good* work in you. Refuse to allow the world to dictate your thoughts and actions. The world will taint your perception but the Lord will enhance it.

    Be bold enough to protect your space, your mind, and your time with God.

3. Build a solid relationship with God. You are in relationship with others, some who do nothing but drain your energy. Choose to be in relationship with The One who grants you peace. The One who is always a benefit to your being. An asset to your living. A helper, counselor, comforter, merciful Father. The relationship will begin to yield indications of what your purpose is and who is leading, guiding, protecting you along the way, your Heavenly Father.

Stay committed to solidifying the relationship you share.

Seek Him and you will find Him. We must seek in order to find. If we do not seek we will not find. If you have ever played hide and seek you know the seeker does not stay in one spot, they go on a search for the hiders. They would never be found if you did not go searching for them (unless they had a great hiding spot and were tired of waiting to be found). The perk here is when we go on a search for God we do not have to look very far. God is not the MVP at hide and seek (He could be if He wanted to). Rather, He chooses to be the hider in the most obvious spot like behind the thinnest tree. You know the hider who you question whether they were even hiding in the first place. Could they have picked a more obvious spot to "hide"? Were they being lazy? Was it a lack of time to find a more adequate spot? Either way, when you yourself are bigger than the tree you are hiding behind the seeker is likely to spot you a mile away. Maybe not a mile away but you get my point. God is like the hider behind the thinnest tree. He is not actually hiding from us. He wants to be found which makes the seeking much easier. When you seek Him do it with every ounce you have and He will be found every single time. He longs for you to find Him. To search for Him with all your heart.

> *But from there you will seek the Lord your*
> *God, and you will find Him if you seek Him*

> *with all your heart and with all your soul.*
> *Deuteronomy 4:29*

The more we seek Him the more we find Him. The dilemma is evident when we neglect to seek God. Continuously. Wholeheartedly. How annoying to go through all the trouble of hiding in a good spot, let alone an obvious place and the seeker never comes to find you. Effort, whether little or great will be all for nothing if we do not seek who or what we are looking for. If we do not seek Him, we will never fully uncover what He has already gifted to us. We have been gifted. Prized by God to be the carrier of extraordinary. To activate our gifts, we must pursue Him and while in pursuit He will unravel our purpose. The closer the seeker gets to the hider it becomes clearer where the seeker needs to go. Sometimes we question whether we are going in the right direction. Sometimes we walk by it many times without an awareness of its existence. When we seek we must open our eyes and ears because most times what is "hiding" will reveal itself on its own. Let us not bask in our insecurities, limit our capability, or give up too soon when we are in the vicinity of our blessing; steps away from what we are seeking.

Every stage presents us with an opportunity to unwrap the paper, to tear off another piece of the gift wrap and discover another portion of God's blessing for our lives. ***The pursuit unravels the purpose.*** Once you begin unveiling pieces of your purpose you will also gain discernment to sift through what needs to go or stay. The wrapping may be pretty and I have known some people who keep the paper to re-gift for later which may be cost effective but some things are not always salvageable. Some things served a purpose before but it just will not measure up for where you are going.

I tend to go through my closet at least once a year, if not more, to rid myself of things that no longer appeal to me. Either it's too tight, too bright, or not my style of choice anymore. In this removal of things that once had a place in my space, I now make room for things that will be a better fit for me. It may have measured up before and suited me well back then but it has become a bit restrictive now, and less appealing, and what once was pretty to look at has become a hindrance to my growth. So, what you may have thought was about clothes has become a process for me. A process of renewal, to allow God to replenish my heart, mind, and soul. He cannot replenish, He cannot fill me up if I am already full. I go through this process because I yearn to be filled up by God and not filled up by things. Once you expose what is underneath the façade and seek to delve into it a bit further, to learn from it, then you will grow. You will recognize what to welcome in and what to escort out. There are some things or some people who get in but need to get out. Activate the power in you. It is up to you whether or not to receive the wisdom of God. Such wisdom will give you the authority to create balance within your life. It is freely given to those willing and ready to accept it.

> *For the Lord gives wisdom; from His*
> *mouth come knowledge and understanding;*
> *Proverbs 2:6*

It is our assignment to accept what has been given to us and take what we have and present it to the world. We must absorb these things into our spirit to fully receive the blessings of God. With knowledge and understanding there is growth which breeds opportunity.

You were never created to be ordinary but rather extraordinary. You have to be willing to work passionately toward bringing out what is inside of you in order to do mighty works. Your perception is critical because it requires faith to look beyond where you currently are to where you want to be. How you perceive yourself solidifies your walk on this earth. Whether you will walk the walk and talk the talk or do one or the other. He has created each individual with a specific goal in mind and most times it goes unnoticed. We limit ourselves and God when we fail to realize the wealth of our being. The bounty of Our Creator. The ability of our mind.

We have to rebuke what the enemy says about us because it is untrue. I know what God says about me. I know He thinks highly of me. I understand He made me so marvelously and nothing I or you do or say can refute this fact.

> *I will praise You, for I am fearfully and*
> *wonderfully made; marvelous are Your*

works, and that my soul knows very well.
Psalm 139:14

Our soul knows how marvelous His works are. We as human beings are His works; therefore, we are marvelous. It can be difficult grasping this, our individual worth, when people are coming up against us spewing the opposite of this. It is then when we have to remind ourselves, our mind, what our spirit is already aware of. Your haters may not know His works are marvelous so you may have to remind them through scripture and if they still do not want to believe it, move on. You played your part. Let those who hate you motivate you to delve deeper into His love and truth. Do not stop speaking the word of God because of what the naysayers say. Remind them, and remind yourself, whose you are. I belong to the Most High, the One True God, The Potter and Sculptor of the heavens and earth. ***If you know who and whose you are the enemies coming for you will flee from you.*** When you know yourself you will not accept defeat because you understand your abilities are maximized by His power.

No weapon formed against you shall prosper,
and every tongue which rises against you in
judgment You shall condemn... Isaiah 54:17

The plan(s) of the enemy to take you out will not work. The word tells us, no weapon. Not some weapons, maybe a few, nope. No weapon. Formed against you. Shall prosper. It does not say they will not form but it does say it will not succeed in taking you out. Your ability to fulfill the purpose within you is far greater than any obstacle ahead. Even the chatter of your critics will become insignificant because you were built to last. We must keep our mind stayed on Jesus. Enduring until the end. If we keep our focus on completing the assignment at hand, God will sustain us.

The Lord shall preserve you from all evil; He shall preserve your soul. Psalms 121:7

You will be shielded from all the enemy attempts to throw at you because God provides the greatest level of protection. Defending not only your body but your spirit. He provides full protection. You may have a few bumps and bruises but your spirit will be unscathed, in fact, it will be strengthened. We thought public figures heavily guarded by a team of security were something special, but at this point we should begin to realize our own exceptionalism. He is on guard. Think for a moment of all the things you have been protected from. All of the things you have been able to withstand. All of the things seeking to devour you, yet you are still here. Some things you may not even have known you were saved from but God's hand is covering you because He wants to see His purpose for you come into fruition. He will not give up and neither should you.

—

Confidence is a trait you must possess in order to

truly embrace your being. You can exude confidence without arrogance. There is not a need to gloat about the possession but the possessor deserves praise and being a confident child of God is honoring Him. Your self-assurance will draw others to you simply due to your belief. I tweak the term slightly to reflect what it means to me to be a confident child of God. Godfident individuals walk boldly in who they are. To be Godfident one eludes to knowing, understanding, and acquiring wisdom of not only oneself alone but of God's presence within them. We need to know and understand His workings, His strategies, and intricacies to better understand our own functionality; what we have to offer in this time and season of life.

I was taught from a young age to be who I am and respect who others are too. My mother would wake me by saying "Good morning, pretty, proud, strong, little, black girl, and I would chime in as she said "Momma's little bundle of joy." It was early in life when I recognized how meaningful I was. I knew I held value, especially from my parents and my brothers. I was the only girl and the baby of the family; the youngest of three, so I always was (and continue to be) protected. With daddy wrapped around my finger and two older brothers sheltering me from danger or what they deemed to be dangerous, like other boys, I was at an advantage. They wanted to protect their little sister because we were taught to protect one another from harm. As the older brothers, they had a duty to defend me, and each other, or suffer the consequences if anyone ended up hurt in any way. Many times, I was introduced as "Edley's little sister" rather than Alyssa so you knew what you were up against. Looking back now I laugh, I guess at the time it was probably a good thing scaring all the boys away. Their intimidating role as 'big brother' probably saved me from some unnecessary heartbreaks.

With age, I began to realize their protection was only part of it. I have a greater level of protection from God. I could see His hand covering me in many areas of my life, especially in relationships. It was not until much later, high school and college days, when I decided the timing was more suitable to date. I have been in a couple relationships and in each instance, I was the one who ended things. The love was present but once it lacked reciprocity I could no longer stay put. In each case I probably stayed longer than I should have due to my "never give up" spirit but God had given me the discernment to make a move or else I would put myself through more unwanted pain. I remained confident in the plan for my life. What was for me was for me and whatever felt like it no longer belonged I had to let go. It was an epiphany and it made it easier for me to move on with no regrets because there was a reason it happened how it happened when it happened. I understood the value of the moments and the value of the not yets. At some point, there was mutual value and effort demonstrated which made the process of an ending to a new beginning an easier transition.

I began to see how all relationships are not long lasting, some relationships end. Whether it be by choice or not. It can be difficult when relationships expected to last come to an end (and I am not just referring to boyfriends here). Growing up we were taught if we start something we have to finish it. Initially, it was hard for me to step away from people because I thought I was giving up, which would go against my values. Revaluating certain situations, I began to understand the end does not indicate personal defeat, but rather a fulfillment of your role.

What I could and can always count on is the love of God to sustain me throughout my growing process. It is an unending process and I am dependent upon Him in support of my growth and His glory. His love is always present. It was this agape, selfless, sacrificial, unconditional, all-encompassing love which taught me the value of life. The authority one can possess over oneself to express love, one to another, as we were sent here to do. You may want to consider removing anything lacking a genuine feel as not to depreciate in value. You do not want to be tied to the enemy. To be your best self you must reject what is inhibiting optimal functionality. You have to dismiss pessimism and project confidence. It was my upbringing, the teaching of values, which awakened me to what I am most compassionate about which is positively impacting others through faith, love, and authenticity. Each one sets the foundation to build up the world we live in.

I am aware we were brought up differently. In different households and different neighborhoods but the goal remains the same, to love one another as God loves us. Live out your expression of love. Discover your personal value. Love yourself then love others. The only reinforcement of love and protection you should seek is from The One (and I am not referring to a partner). I am referring to God. It may not be a mother or father telling you how important you are; it may be a stranger offering a compliment but if they are MIA (missing in action) seek GOD for affirmation, confirmation, revelation, vindication. Thank God for your supporters but when no one else is around to cheer for you, cheer for yourself. Treat yourself as the prize you are. Take yourself to the movies. Wine and dine on your own dime. His timing is perfect. His presence is endless. Above all else, be confident in Him.

2

TIMING IS EVERYTHING

As the clock ticks insist on ingesting more of yourself.

Every day is an opportunity to learn something new about yourself. It takes a lifetime to grow into who you truly are but what a privilege to get acquainted with yourself.

Over time you begin to appreciate your flaws. Your imperfections bring out your uniqueness and your individuality is one of your biggest attractions. For the rest of your life you will be on a journey discovering more about you. The environmental and situational changes will produce growth; spiritually, mentally, emotionally, and physically. In the midst of maturation, you begin to understand the purposeful processes. To uncover the hidden potential inside of you it is vital to act upon the nudging, the recurring creative thoughts, the desire to do more. You have to unwrap your gift, opening yourself up to embrace the present within. What is inside holds the real treasure.

The discovery and reveal of your gift is when you truly begin to see God's Hand. Giving glory to the one who granted you stewardship over your gift by maximizing it. Unwrapping and sharing it with others. **God is the epitome of the gift and the gifter.** He, Himself, is a gift for all to receive but He does not stop there. He gifts us with more than His presence, He gifts us presents. Presents he has molded within us with the intention of making a difference in the lives of others. He knows what is inside of us and the importance of bearing the gift for others to receive. He looks forward to the moment when we realize what He has known all along, we are gifts to the world. Prophets, Preachers, Teachers, Motivators,

Mentors, Disciples in our many roles as Daughters, Sons, Sisters, Brothers, Mothers, Fathers, Aunts, Uncles, Cousins, and Friends. We may be able to fool other people into thinking "we are not that" but we cannot fool God. Frankly, we all have some work to do in exposing our internal beauty with our external facade. Learning how to fully embrace our gift and share in the gifting.

It is nice to have a put together exterior but if the interior is falling apart there is work to be done. I know you have heard them say 'everything that glitters is not gold'. We have to focus on being golden and not simply looking it. There is a profound difference between looking the part and being the part. A lot more effort goes into being. This is the time where you either push forward or give up due to the pressure. Being who we were created to be is a tough task because of adversity. Some of us are fearful of exposing what lies on the inside because it may not match up to our expectations – or theirs.

They may not respond to your gifting. They liked you more when you were wrapped up. Yet, your wrapping did not reveal the real, true, unveiled you. The wrapping only served as an indication of a gift. It would be difficult to wrap air, of no substance, therefore the wrapping signifies what lies within. You have something significant inside of you waiting to be unraveled. There is a time to wait in your wrapping, to let it be known that there is a gift inside but then comes the grand reveal. Fear of the opinion of others makes us believe our gift is not a grand reveal but I am here to tell you that it is. At times we wait with anticipation to unravel and other times we rip through the paper a bit too soon. I can say the latter was my preference when I was younger and my brain was less developed as I'm sure it was for you too. I still have moments where I prefer the latter but am disciplined enough to know some things take time. Either way, it is worth uncovering. Once we understand the importance of exposing what lies within we are less concerned with what others think or say and more aware of what God says.

> *As each one has received a gift, minister it to one another, as good stewards of the manifold grace of God. If anyone speaks, let him speak as the oracles of God. If anyone ministers, let him do it as with the ability which God supplies, that in all things God may be glorified through Jesus Christ, to whom belong the glory and the dominion forever and ever. Amen. 1 Peter 4:10-11*

Our gift is not for us alone. We possess it and we must minister it to others. We do not have to be preachers to minister to someone. In fact, 1 Peter 4:10 is instructing us to share our gifts with others as a testament to God's grace. It does not specify one person is more gifted than another and they should share but you should not. No, it states, *each one has received, minister it to one another.* Clearly suggesting those who have received should be ministering what has been received to someone else. I know ministering can be an intimating term so to put it simply ministering is to tend to the needs of someone.

In essence, we are to use our gift to inspire. Your gift is meaningful and, in most cases, necessary for someone else's breakthrough. It is rarely ever just about you because it extends beyond you as an illustration of God's grace toward you and available for others. Wow.

Verse 11 further instructs us. We are His vessels if we allow ourselves to be open to His utilization. He gives us the ability to allow our gift to tend to someone else. He does so with the intention to glorify God even further. If we grant Him access, He will reign. His dominion over our lives ensures His protection. Simply, because He is ours and we our His we can triumph over whatever the enemy attempts to throw our way. Under the pressure of stressors our light will continue to shine because we know not only who is on our side but also what He has equipped us with.

> *I called on the Lord in distress; the Lord answered me, and set me in a broad place. The Lord is on my side; I will not fear. What can man do to me? Psalm 118: 5-6*

We are not made to fear man but if the fear arises remember who is on your side. Remember who is fighting for you. We just have to make the call and once the call is made His power will promote you. He takes us from a small arena to a larger arena, enlarging our territory along the way. Equipping us for each season. By calling on Him we acknowledge whose team we are on. Team Jesus. The winning team. With the Lord on our side there is no room for fear to take up the bench. His authority alone causes us to perk up a bit more because His power is exuded in us. We can confidently go in the direction of our calling because the Lord answers every call. He knows who we are at our core. He knows what we are made of but we could use a reminder from time to time. I greatly appreciate those. Those God-confirming, revelation-invoking, spirit-stirring words. We cannot look to the outer appearance and be completely satisfied without digging deeper and focusing in on the central part of our functionality – our heart. *We must discover what makes us tick and allow our ticking to influence the tock of others.* Our hearts are our source of life creating connection internally to our body's functions and externally to others. When we are active in our faith, ministering, speaking, and glorifying God our hearts are operating in their potential.

It is our inactivity that leads to ineffectiveness. When we stop digging deeper and expressing our gift in its rawest, most genuine form we are becoming unproductive. Unfortunately, we allow many things to get in the way of pursing God's Will. A big distraction comes from the opinion of others causing some of us to halt in our tracks. Making us reconsider if this is the route we should take. Let me stop to encourage you: if their attraction stops at the glitter, the outward appearance, your gift is not meant for them. Until you pierce further than the eye can see, to the heart, you will be blinded by their limited views.

We have to breach the system. We have to break through to what is on the other side of our comfort zone. Bulldoze through the wall of acceptance from people and aim for acceptance from God. Until we confront what is beyond the exterior we will never encounter the full effect of what we have to offer in this present time. The problem is not being unaware of our potential because with time and effort we will be made aware. The problem is when we become alert to the possibilities of what we should be doing, the impact we should be having, the lives we should see changing (including our own), instead of excitement, we hesitate. We get nervous. Scared.

We are people pleasers. Living in a world where we are more receptive to how other people perceive us, which limits our own perspective. Understand, you can be mindful of what people say without allowing their opinions of you to dictate who you are. Your opinion is yours, and everyone is entitled to one. It can be heard without being accepted. It is okay to receive feedback as long as you channel it into your growing process. Otherwise, it can be destructive giving others the power to influence you because if you do not walk boldly in who you are, in your gifting, you may lose yourself along the way. The disadvantage then is not exposing the true you to others. You are too elaborate to sacrifice yourself in order to appeal to a restricted, inside the box, version.

We must move beyond the approval of others by completely embracing ourselves. By letting our light shine. I know you have heard the song "this little light of mine" especially if you have ever experienced vacation bible school but singing about your light and actually letting it shine are very different. We do not have to know the how's and why's of it all we just need to shine.

Gratefully, we serve a God who knows what we do not know. Anytime we are feeling the need for some feedback, some reassurance, some encouragement before we pick up the phone to call (or text) our sisters or brothers in Christ call the Lord first. He knows what we do not know and with Him our call will be answered every time with a reply intended to enlighten us.

> *'Call to me, and I will answer you, and show you great and mighty things, which you do not know.' Jeremiah 33:3*

If you make the call, He will pick up. I know I am talking in the context of a phone but you do not need a physical phone, you just need to speak to Him. Have a conversation with Him and He will respond. I will pause to say He may not respond in the way you thought or the way you wanted. He has a lot to say but He can say it in many different ways through many different means. If you want to hear from Him make yourself available to Him and wait patiently for Him. You have something inside of you He wants to show to the world whether you know it or not. Whether you are fully aware of what you have or not, there is a light internally that needs to shine externally. If you get caught up in what you do not know, you will not be capable of shining. When you get caught up you begin to doubt yourself and there is no room for doubt.

To let our light shine, to touch people spiritually, we have to be vulnerable enough to reach out to Him. He will show us great things. Bit by bit and piece by piece He will reveal our unknowns; providing revelation to what has been lying dormant in our soul for far too long. It is up to us to make the initial contact. Inaction will never yield the results we anticipate. We have to do and become. We must recognize how our action invokes the action of others. Actively seeking to be what we know we are because what we do is in some way related to what others will do. Your action is tied to someone else's blessing. In return, by being a blessing you will also be blessed.

> *But be doers of the word, and not hearers*
> *only, deceiving yourselves. James 1:22*

Doers, do. It is an action word. Read The Word, hear The Word, but do what The Word is telling you. If you only receive it with your eyes and ears you miss the opportunity to walk in it, own it, and sustain it. They say practice what you preach, implicating a need to apply an idea or belief by performance. To be a doer requires effort and execution in order to complete the task at hand. You cannot be a light to others if you are not a light unto yourself. You cannot convince others of your wisdom if you are unconvinced. Encourage yourself, speak life over yourself and soon enough you will be doing the same for others. Allow your actions to speak for you but evaluate what you do and say along the way.

Ask yourself (and God):

1. What is hindering me from becoming the best version of myself?

    There are people, places, and things to cut from your daily routine in order to reach this new and improved self. I know it is uncomfortable to picture life from a different lens but until you face your discomfort you will remain grounded, unable to elevate to your potential. If there is any hindrance to your development you should reconsider its position. Not to say you should start eliminating things from your life entirely but you may want to put some distance between what is causing you to wither and move closer to what is stimulating your growth.

2. What steps are being taken to unleash my full potential?

    You have to be accountable for where you are to get to where you want to go. If you need to write it down and read it every day, do whatever it takes to commit to crossing stuff off the list and accomplishing the rest. I am a writer so I have journals everywhere. Inside are notes, goals, steps, prayers, and rants all in attempt to keep me accountable. I revisit them to see what I was thinking, what ideas I was birthing, whether I am closer or further from where I intended and whether it was realistic. Beyond that, whether it was in alignment with God's plan. Not about me or others but Him. You do not want to fall into the trap of comparing what someone else is doing to what you are doing (or should be doing). ***Comparison is only a distraction to your action.*** If it works and brings you closer to Jesus do it but if not, reevaluate.

3. What is triggering the power within me?

There should be someone or something encouraging, motivating, and strengthening you. Hone in on it, whatever 'it' is. Whoever it is. You ought to have some driving force enabling you to push past the adversity. You cannot do this alone. God did not design us that way. For a season, maybe but not for a lifetime. Let Him use others to feed your spirit to move forward to your desired destination. Cheering you on to live on purpose in His purpose.

Once you have thought on these things, review them, write them down, and act upon them. Action is your demonstration of the direction in which you want to advance. Forward or backward. Continue to propel onward and rid yourself of anything or anyone who is keeping you restricted.

Never allow anyone to make you feel inadequate. God will use you despite your mistakes and failures. I live with a goal of not making the same mistake twice but rather learning from every experience by pulling the good from it. If anything, it should have taught you (and others) what not to do. Often, an individual experience is mutually experienced. A lot of situations could be avoided or approached differently if those who have already been through it spoke about their breakthrough. It is worth expressing our experiences because acknowledgement can bring someone else out of a dire situation or prevent it entirely. We have to stop living in shame from what we have done in the past. If God is over it, we need to get over it. He showers us with grace and mercy because He knows we are going to mess up, yet He still shows compassion.

> *He is ever merciful, and lends; and His descendants are blessed. Psalms 37:26*

We are His seed. Therefore, we are blessed. Find comfort in knowing God has mercy on us. Just ask for it. He has compassion and forgiveness for you. Nothing you have been through is too much for Him not to reveal His grace and mercy towards you. You went through it but you were not consumed by it. There is a reason why you are still here whether you believe it or not. Let Him be the judge of your life, not anyone else. Do not abort the mission because of what they say, listen to what He is instructing you to do. Your significance is too great to let anything get in the way of your purpose. You have a job to do. You have a purpose to fulfill. You must rise up and go in the direction of your calling. Nobody can do it for you. It is dependent upon your own functionality. You have to work it like never before.

> *Now to Him who is able to do exceedingly*
> *abundantly above all that we ask or think,*
> *according to the power that works in us,*
> *Ephesians 3:20*

It is up to us. Our power. Our action. Our efforts. We have to put the work in. If we are not ready for the benefits it is only a reflection of our own disbelief. He cannot just place it in our life if we are not prepared for it. We are simply holding up the process. In the meantime, God has other things to concern himself with. He is not a one-person God. We may have time to waste but God has souls to save, lives to protect, mouths to feed, angels to dispatch, and He tends to those who are committed to the mission; who love Him, and seek Him diligently.

When you are ready to resume the mission, He will be there. He knows which way you should go but He allows you to go in the direction you see fit in order for you to grow from every experience. Sometimes our choice leads to more growing pains than intended but that does not stop Him from allowing us to choose our path. In fact, He knows which path you will choose. Whether it be the path of least resistance is up to you. You may be tired and tried, you may be bruised up, but when you come out of it you will be as pure as gold. Notice I said when you come out, not if.

> *But he knows the way that I take; when*
> *He has tested me, I shall come forth as gold.*
> *Job 23:10*

Every wrong turn or detour is necessary to maneuver to the next task, the next step, the next challenge, and the next blessing. The strain you encounter builds strength. The bumps, peaks, and valleys are a part of your route to triumph. I believe every single thing happens for a reason. This reason should motivate us to maneuver through whatever comes up against us because it is this pressing through that forms solid gold. **The process presents the opportunity.**

When we are tested we are able to demonstrate our progression, our knowledge, what we have learned along the way. Sometimes it hurts to press through where you once were into where you are intended to be. It requires you to stay committed to your calling because if God called you to it, He will comfort you through it. You are bred for this. As long as you keep your mind on it and your actions towards obtaining it you will be successful at carrying out the mission set before you. He will reward your effort if effort is what you give Him. Show Him how determined you are to not only survive, but thrive in this season and watch how He elevates you.

You cannot simply exist. If existence was all we had to do we would have all reached our objective by now. Instead, we must stretch our parameters, broaden our perspectives, and extend our reach. We must critique our stride every step of the way so we are minimizing our missteps and staying on pace. We have to be motivated to move beyond where we once were comfortable and elevate to a new level of comfortability. At times finding comfort in the unfamiliar and the uncertainties of life. We may not be certain of our environment or our current circumstances but we can always be certain of God's presence in the midst of it all.

> *Have I not commanded you? Be strong and of a good courage; do not be afraid, nor be dismayed, for the Lord your God is with you wherever you go. Joshua 1:9*

It takes courage to grow and be strong. It is courageous of you to challenge your mind to push past its limitations. Imagine thinking the same thoughts, or staying at the same level you were on as a child – it becomes limited. With age comes growth and you determine what you tolerate. You must evaluate what is impacting your growing process and set the necessary guidelines. God will not promote you if you do not want to advance. If you do not want to be transformed you will not be. When you are sick and tired of the same ole same, willing to grow, ready to show yourself approved then you will move closer to your calling. You have to prepare yourself for progression. It is not something that can be obtained without putting in the time and effort. Once you take the step He will pave the way but first you must take the step. The action indicates the faith, once displayed, you have raised the bar. There is a sense of excitement once you up the ante because He operates best on higher levels of thinking, moving, and evolving. His elevated level of thinking and moving can propel you to heights far greater than before.

> *"For My thoughts are not your thoughts, nor are your ways My ways," says the Lord. "For as the heavens are higher than the earth, so are My ways higher than your ways, and My thoughts than your thoughts." Isaiah 55:8-9*

Although He is higher than us, He can always be reached by us. We must strive to acquire His wisdom by expanding our thinking and diving deeper into His Word. We must aim higher when it comes to our thoughts and actions. Yet, always be willing to grow from the challenge even if it comes with failure. Welcoming every opportunity to upgrade our thoughts, actions, and reactions. We all could benefit from advancement if the steps are taken in proper order. We only have to be open to newness and excited to explore our unknowns that are known by God.

Your purpose is linked to an aspect of you not yet discovered. Once you find it, embrace it, because it will lead you into new realms, new opportunities, and new relationships. As much as your purpose is about you it is not only about you. For to obtain the blessings it will yield is not a benefit for only you to receive. You must share what is God-given in order to bring people to Him, to glorify His holy name.

> *Let your light so shine before men, that they*
> *may see your good works and glorify your*
> *Father in heaven. Matthew 5:16*

The scripture is telling us our light causes others to exalt Him. Our light allows them to see. If we let our light shine before men, our good works will be seen and God will be praised. You have no idea the magnitude of your blessing. It is much broader than you could ever imagine. God works on a large scale, a grand scale. He knows the ripple effect of one blessed soul to another results in a chain reaction. We are presented with opportunities to be a witness to others. Blessing souls and glorifying God in the process.

Let's build and support one another, speaking life and love over each other. Encouraging and uplifting the world to be a bit brighter than before without the expectation of something in return. No one will be left untouched if we activate what is contained in the depths of our being. Our Loving Father is rooting for us.

—

I was brought up in the church, attending on many days and evenings throughout the week. It was an enjoyment of mine to be in the house of God (most of the time). Part of it may have been the freedom of running around the sanctuary with the other kids while the adults conversed in the back after service. Maybe it was attending Sunday School to learn about "this little light of mine". It could have been participating in the church plays or singing in the children's choir. Even the outreach services we offered in the preparation and delivery of meals to hungry souls or the bake sales (every kind of pastry you could imagine) or even the clothes drives. More importantly, the satisfaction could have come from the moments of preaching in which, as a child, I was able to comprehend the true power of who God was. Instilling moments of excited compassion in giving back to others as a glimpse into my purpose of encouraging, tending, and shining light into the life of another.

Growing up in the church allowed me to open my mind to sacrificial giving. In total admiration of Our God. In praising, in offering, in worship, it was owed to Him. I must add there was a lot of praise dancing at Greater Bethel. No quenching of The Holy Spirit there. In fact, I would mimic the praisers and preacher from time to time (Lord, forgive me). I may not have understood completely but He was sowing seeds and there were moments where I felt the peace of His presence from the seeds that were sown back then. The praise was an expression of gratitude for His faithfulness and there are many ways you can show your appreciation. Not everyone praises in the same way and it is okay, as long as you praise Him. My mom reminded me how we are such cheerleaders for our sports team and in the same way we root for our teams, we too can cheer for God. You stand, clap, stomp, and shout for a sports team and you can do all of those things for God. You do not go to a game and stare at the crowd, you go to a game to watch those who are performing and root for them. You have to ignore what the crowd is doing and embrace the performer.

As a young child, I did not care too much what people thought. As a teen, I shied away from praising because of what "they" may think. Now you will hear the yes's and amen's as I feel an inclination in my spirit or you may see me wave my hand or open my arms in surrender of His Spirit. I will no longer allow someone else's opinion of my praise to stop me from embracing Him. He has been too good to me for me not to thank Him. It is what is due to Him. It brings a smile to my face to see true worshippers acknowledging and glorifying God.

I was baptized at the age of 9. Although I was only a child the symbolism of what it meant to be baptized in the name of the Father, the Son, and the Holy Spirit resonated in my soul. It set the standard for how I wanted to live my life in alignment with Him. I was re-baptized at the age of 23 as a rededication of my life in adulthood to Him. There was a lot of life experience from that 9-year-old little girl to that 23-year-old woman. God had always been a part of me but now I wanted to demonstrate to Him my eagerness for Him to consume all of me. I needed His leadership. I began seeking His presence diligently in order to understand why I was set apart from everyone else. To understand what my God-given purpose was and pursue it wholeheartedly. Prior to my recommitment at 23, He continued to give me words to write. Most times I thought it was more for me than anything or anyone else but He was compiling those words into this book you are reading.

I was not a perfect child, with a perfect family, who never made mistakes. Nor am I a perfect adult either. At some point, we all have sinned and come short of the glory of God (Romans 3:23). The question then is how did I recover from my wrongs? Quite simply, by recognizing the issue and adjusting my behavior from there. Conviction is the term used but I obviously did not know it then. I just understood right from wrong and would act accordingly but nothing was wasted. I have always been a quick learner (expect for Math, that took additional hours of tutoring and I still struggled but I made it through – Praise God). As a child, if I did not quickly learn from my poor choice my mother would gladly assist which would cause me to snap out of it real quick. I knew I was capable of doing better and being better and worked to master knowing better in efforts to improve the doing and being. I still slip up on occasion but I know whose I am and I live for Him.

Once I differentiated between what was acceptable and unacceptable from my mother I was able to understand the power of discipline. Beginning to feel convicted whenever I knew I was doing something which would cause disapproval. In comparison to being disciplined by a parent, God also disciplines (some of us would prefer the discipline of our parents versus the correction we receive from God). Either way, the punishment is meant to serve as a correction and redirection toward a desired behavior. They want to keep us en route to becoming all we can be. Praising optimal functionality but first establishing structure. The correction would only come when I was off track. There is no need for discipline when you are doing what you are supposed to do. No need to correct an acceptable behavior. A reward may be a result of good behavior in order to influence your incentive to continue such but discipline surely follows unwanted behavior.

The moment I committed a violation of the rules, I was quickly rerouted. The path I chose took me off route but also lead me to where I went astray so I could correct the misstep. As long as you are following the route there is no need to express concern or regain order but once you make the wrong move be ready for redirection. The good thing about having older siblings is you already have an idea of what to do and what not to do based on the punishment they received. You recognize the repercussions from their actions. I would think to myself, "he was punished for what he did so I will refrain from doing what he did (or else pray I do not get caught doing it)." The bonus then is the example they set. Now, not all of their examples are good to adopt but a sibling who genuinely loves you wants the best for you and tends to voice their wisdom when it matters most. I had to refrain from what I knew blocked the path of my destiny. With God ordering my steps, along with what I had been instilled with growing up I was on my way to discovering the uniqueness of where God was taking me.

I was a happy child. Always active, always compassionate. I had to keep up with my brothers somehow. They had the 'if you can't play with the big boys, stay on the porch' mentality and I wanted to play with the big boys. My agility as a child motivated me to compete in track and field but my supportive nature influenced my cheerleading spirit. I was a cheerleader from peewee all the way through high school. I know they come with a stigma of being preppy, mean girls but I was not the type. I tried to be a friend to everybody and cheer for everybody. I was a huge fan. Rooting for your success and yelling for you to get your head in the game. Always encouraging people to put their best foot forward. I have always felt inclined to inspire people to reach their full potential and show my admiration for their efforts. Being supportive was important to me but being supported also became equally as important.

In 7th grade, I began track and field and stuck with it through my 4th year of college (10 years of running is a long time if you ask me, at this point it has become a lifestyle). My participation in track is what greatly influenced my determination. It helped me to see what I was capable of. There were a lot of victories but there was also defeat, and in the face of adversity I had to learn how to rise to the challenge. It taught me more about myself than the sport itself because I was challenged physically and mentally. If I could convince my mind I could convince my body and it was this desire to be the best me which also carried over into academics. I maintained good grades because I wanted to be eligible to compete but also because I could not be proud of a C, D, or F. There is something it did to my pride to see anything other than an A or B on a report card. I held myself to a higher standard because I knew the value of accountability. Being responsible for my thoughts, feelings, and actions because if I was in charge of those things I could better myself and inspire others in the process. With age and experience I allowed myself to evolve; taking each step necessary to bring out my spiritual desire. Always remembering to follow what I was most compassionate about because my passion was tied to my purpose. Fortunately, there were indicators but the indicators did not have a shining sign pointing to my exact purpose. Each season of life allowed me to learn, prepare, fail, and try again. All moving me closer to Him.

YOUR DESIRE IS REQUIRED

3.

YOU ARE GIFTED

The spark ignites the blaze but you must maintain the flame.

When we feel the burning desire for more we must not snuff it out. The very reason we are feeling it serves as an indication of our capacity to preserve the blaze versus smothering it as we tend to do. The intention of our potential was not that it be bottled up for ourselves but rather brought out for others to see.

It is no good to be gifted but hide your giftedness. Your gift demands presentation. It wants to be shown off. Presented. Offered as a blessing to someone else. It serves as a demonstration of your faith. An attraction to draw others to the main attraction. God did not anoint you for it with the expectation that you would fail to use it. This is why you are constantly being reminded of your capabilities. You are given signs of the gifts in you in order to continually work to cultivate and grow them. Whatever they are, God put them specifically inside of you with a purpose to see them reach their potential. There is a reason those creative thoughts, innovative ideas, and unique designs continuously consume space in your brain.

> *Therefore I remind you to stir up the gift of God which is in you through the laying on of my hands. 2 Timothy 1:6*

Other versions allude to fanning into flame the gifts of God.

God will send all the resources necessary to see His gift of you come into light. Constantly reminding you of your mission but also the obligation to feed it. You have to feed the flame so it will burn on and not out. Once you begin planning and implementing strategies to send this spark blazing God will back you up. He is right there with you feeding the fire, throwing in wood, fulfilling the need. He rewards your action by stoking the flame with all essentials while allowing some things to be consumed. You may have been concerned about what you were losing throughout your progression. The good news is if it was holding you down it had to be removed so you could be lifted back up into your rightful position. Some things have to burn up in the flames but if it be of God, He will always deliver. I cannot think of a more appropriate depiction of His ability to save and display His authority than the three amigos.

Shadrach, Meshach, and Abednego can testify to God's power in sustaining you through the flames. If you recall their account, the king had his men throw them into a burning furnace because, as servants of God, they refused to bow down to the king and his graven images. The heat was so intense the guards who bound them and threw them in died. Yet, Shadrach, Meshach, and Abednego were in the midst of the flames and God was with them, protecting them. The king being a witness to God's power, condemned anyone who spoke against Him, and promoted the three men.

> *…Then Shadrach, Meshach, and Abednego*
> *came from the midst of the fire. And satraps,*
> *administrators, governors, and the king's*
> *counselors gathered together, and they saw*

> *these men on whose bodies the fire had*
> *no power; the hair of their head was not*
> *singed nor were their garments affected,*
> *and the smell of fire was not on them.*
> *Nebuchadnezzar spoke, saying, "Blessed*
> *be the God of Shadrach, Meshach, and*
> *Abednego, who sent His angel and delivered*
> *His servants who trusted in Him, and they*
> *have frustrated the king's word, and yielded*
> *their bodies, that they should not serve nor*
> *worship any god except their own God!"*
> *Daniel 3:26-28*

Trusting Him completely results in the receipt of His benefits. The men who threw them into the flames were not recipients of His benefits. God could have saved them but instead they were consumed by the flames because they did not give Him any authority; they worshiped false gods. There are some things God will allow to be burnt up. ***The flame is intended to burn but based on who you trust it will either burn you or bless you.*** It was clear to see who He had His hands on in the midst of this fiery situation.

Seeing the king's men burnt up, yet Shadrach, Meshach, and Abednego were unscathed, illustrated the all-consuming power of God. The king was a witness to the mighty God these three men served. It was not until he saw this with his own eyes, and confirmed it with his men, that he fully understood and acknowledged their God, and promoted them. ***God will cause the people***

who are plotting against you to promote you. Even when it looks like a losing battle. A situation you may not come out of. If you put your full faith, your full trust in Him, He will take what looks like a loss and turn it into a victory for your enemies to see. It may look like a loss if you are not looking with your faith eyes, but once you activate your faith you welcome the victory. What these three men had done is such a commendable representation of unwavering faith. Refusing to bow down to serve any other God than their own. The One, True, God. So much so, they defy King Nebuchadnezzar. A man who put many others to death without a second thought. Nebuchadnezzar challenged the three men...

> *Now if you are ready at the time you hear the sound of the horn, flute, harp, lyre, and psaltery, in symphony with all kinds of music, and you fall down and worship the image which I have made, good! But if you do not worship, you shall be cast immediately into the midst of a burning fiery furnace. And who is the god who will deliver you from my hands?" Daniel 3:15*

This seemed like a rhetorical question to me. Not needing an answer, but it did not appear to be so for Shadrach, Meshach, and Abednego. In response to King Nebuchadnezzar's threats they replied:

…"O Nebuchadnezzar, we have no need to answer you in this matter. If that is the case, our God who we serve is able to deliver us from the burning fiery furnace, and He will deliver us from your hand, O king. But if not, let it be known to you, O king, that we do not serve your gods, nor will we worship the gold image which you have set up." Daniel 3:16-18

Now I am not sure what you would do in this situation but it is praiseworthy on so many levels. First, I personally do not know I could have acted on the same level of bravery and faithfulness as these three men (but it is certainly my aim to get on their level). Secondly, to be threaten with death, yet still refer to this man as a king. At that point, I am sure I would have lost all respect for this man's position and king would be the last reference he would have received from me. Lastly, these men were confident yet sacrificial. Saying Our God *can* and *will* deliver us. They knew His ability. They knew He could if He desired to. Yet, they plugged in, even *if* He does not do it. We will never serve your gods or graven images. We will never worship something or someone over Our Father. We will not reduce ourselves to a level far below where we were ever intended to be. We know who Our God is. We know what kind of God we serve. His power is unmatched to the power you place on your gods and images. His wrath will wipe out an entire generation, an entire kingdom. How dare you question Our God.

Those may not have been their exact words but I can bet they were their thoughts. They decided to word them differently in their response to the king but they were convinced of the power only Our God holds. They put their faith on it and God put His hand on them. In the midst of the heated situation He allowed them to keep their cool. How astounded Nebuchadnezzar must have been. To be a witness to *that*, you would have to believe *and* believe he did. His entire perspective changed after that moment. He praised God and promoted Shadrach, Meshach, and Abednego. If this account is not encouragement to put fear aside and place all bets on God I am not sure what else could convince you.

Now, I do not believe you will be thrown into a literal fiery furnace. Do I believe there will be situations, life events, storms, as an attempt to burn and destroy you, yes. It would be a great reminder to recall this account when we experience our own fiery situations. In this remembrance, we are reminded He is in the midst of the storm with us. Fighting for us. Delivering us. Following through for us. Grinning as our enemies promote us as a result of the God we serve.

There were three of them. I am not a bible scholar so do not quote me but I do not believe it was specified they were brothers. I can only assume they were friends. They certainly trusted each other. If a brotherhood was not formed prior to the fire it certainly had to come about after. After experiencing a situation such as they had I'm sure their loyalty to one another was securely established. Probably making them question any relationship that did not resemble the same kind of devotion. One loyal friend can be difficult to come by, let alone two. Two who would be willing to stand with you through the life threating taunts of the enemy. Their relationship acted as yet another testament to the intricacies of God's workmanship. He never intended for us to go at it alone. *But* He also never intended for us to be in relationships in which we are not compatible, whether friendships or partnerships.

> *And the Lord God said, "It is not good that man should be alone; I will make him a helper comparable to him." Genesis 2:18*

Now, I know the Lord gave Adam different creatures and even a woman to keep him company but I am not referring to those things here. Not only did the Lord say it is not good for man to be alone. He also said, I will make him a *helper, comparable,* to him. Meaning, you need help. In addition, I am going to *give* you someone to help you. And, that someone will be *similar* to you. You will be on one accord. Iron sharpening iron. If this is not the case in some of your relationships it may be wise to reconsider.

As you progress, you may want to create distance between yourself and those who are not progressing. ***Those you leave behind may become your biggest critics but it is only because they envy your position rather than support your mission.*** You begin to see the difference between allies and adversaries. Your allies support your growth, fueling your desire. Your adversaries are watching, waiting for you to be consumed by the flames. Refuse to afford them the satisfaction of your defeat. Find yourself some Shadrach's, Meshach's, and Abednego's. Get yourself some friends who are willing to weather the storm with you. The Lord will be sure to equip you with the right ones if you continue to put your trust in Him and possess a willingness to fight through the fear every step of the way.

It is not an easy task to feel the fear and do it anyway. Fear is a big culprit to progression because most times it leaves you immobile. It comes as a thought to intimidate you into thinking you cannot obtain what you seek; you are inadequate, unworthy. Fear tends to turn up the volume in your head and reign there if you allow it to. It can be good if you let it push you onward. If you are struck by fear yet push yourself through it, you will. It is only a problem when you are stagnant in fear. Staying fearful by lingering too long in it is not how we were designed.

> *For God has not given us a spirit of fear; but*
> *of power and of love and of a sound mind.*
> *2 Timothy 1:7*

It is not meant to be an emotion to consume us but fear will surely touch us. ***No one is completely fearless but anyone has the potential to fear less.*** We are capable of reducing, silencing, and dismissing fear from our lives anytime it rears its head. We have authority over fear, doubt, worry, and all the other negative emotions (and positive) but our authority is useless if not utilized.

You have to put it to use. You have to refuse to allow anything to keep you immobile. Anything to take control of you. If you are the gatekeeper only what you permit into your life will enter. Therefore, whatever you grant control will only have as much authority as you give it. Be careful how you disperse such power. It was given to you purposefully, to relinquish it may impact your destination. You cannot allow the asset to become a liability because you failed to utilize and protect it. For those who receive Him also receive His benefits.

> *But as many as received Him, to them He gave the right to become children of God, to those who believe in His name: who were born, not of blood, nor of the will of the flesh, nor of the will of man, but of God. John 1:12-13*

Not everyone receives the power because they do not accept, receive, or believe Him. It would be unwise to give power to someone who is underserving of it. These are teachable moments for God to intercede on your behalf. If you get yourself into something unpleasant His grace will allow you to learn from it and His mercy will allow you to recover.

Do not be afraid of God, however, it is acceptable to be afraid of His actions. His discipline may lead you to be fearful but understand your obedience is what gets you the blessing. If you were not disciplined you would never be blessed. Discipline then allows you to adjust. You cannot change what you did but you can modify your approach. It may have been painful to have gone through it but you learned valuable lessons from it.

> *Now no chastening seems to be joyful for the present, but painful; nevertheless, afterward it yields the peaceable fruit of righteousness to those who have been trained by it. Hebrews 12:11*

What you go through will not always be a joyous occasion but there is always a 'but'. It may not be enjoyable right now, *but*. You may not be happy in this moment, *but*. After you go through it, after you persevere, after it happens, the after indicates an ending. After the chaos, you will receive peace but you will not receive peace until after. You have to go through it. As much as we would like to we cannot bypass the process.

It is okay to be a little afraid. It is okay to be shocked. Questioning how Our Mighty God could use what seems so small to do something so magnificent. It is okay if you cannot fathom His power because it is so immense. It is indescribable. It can be incomprehensible, it can leave you awestruck and if it breeds a bit of fear, it is understandable. Let it spark your interest into discovering how a bit of fear can advance your life.

*The fear of the Lord leads to life and he who
has it will abide in satisfaction; He will not
be visited with evil. Proverbs 19:23*

You fear what you do not know or what you cannot imagine and this fear can be used in your favor. If you fear Him you must also trust Him because if you have fear with no trust He cannot influence your breakthrough. Your trust has to be greater than your fear. If you fear Him but trust His grandiose purpose for your life, you will always be amazed by Him. You will forever be satisfied by His capabilities. You will be impressed by His belief in you. This fear will protect you from evil and trusting Him will leave you satisfied. So, if you are going to fear at all, fear God and His power, but trust His intervention. If He intervenes He will make things happen whether they be pleasant or unpleasant experiences.

No matter the experience progression can only be obtained if you maintain momentum. This is why it is essential to cut off the things tangling you up and reducing your ability to push through. There is no need to revisit limiting moments from your past, you can reflect on the moment to gauge your progress but appreciate the amount of growth that has transpired. You can learn a lot by simply reevaluating the situation.

Ask yourself (and God):

1. Have I been in this position before?
2. How can I experience this similar situation differently and more insightfully?

3. In what way can I use the power in me to maneuver through my current circumstance effectively?
4. What are you attempting to teach me from this situation?

Your reaction is based on your outlook and your outlook determines your endorsement. You have to be careful what you support because if it is not aligned with who you are and what you believe in, your sincerity may be questioned. Now, your sincerity will be questioned either way but if all you are and all you do is true to who you are the scrutiny is insignificant. If you become destiny conscious you can focus your mind on progressive thoughts. You can focus on evolving. Focus on feeding the desires of your heart and less on listening to what he said or she said. ***You choose what you will entertain.*** Each day you choose. You choose how you are going to be affected. You choose how you will allow events of the day to influence your reaction. Whether a situation will taint your perspective or leave you confidently unbothered it is up to you.

You have to embrace the day in a positive manner. Speaking out what you desire and following up with action. What you think has everything to do with where you will go so be aware of every thought you think. Determine what you can do to be effective and do it. Anyone can speak a thing; what matters is how you follow through. You should rely on God but you demonstrate your dedication by backing it with action. Had Shadrach, Meshach, and Abednego said what they said, so confidently and eloquently but just before being thrown into the fire caved, cried, and bowed down to Nebuchadnezzar their story likely would not have been as significant. It would not have revealed the true power of God. Their words said one thing and their actions were in total confidence of what had been said. Total surrender and belief in God. Their follow-through lead to their promotion. Action is fundamental. It seals the deal which is why we have to do. We have to be doers of the Word. If God is working we better be too.

—

I did not invest much time into finding out my true purpose until college. It was as if I was prompted to do more and be more during this season. A bit conflicting as college can be quite demanding, especially being a student-athlete. But it was during this time when I began to invest the time to write. I felt inclined to write. Called to write. It also forced me to recount and fully appreciate the opportunities presented to me (which is why I refrained from the party scene on *most* occasions). Not to say that I never attended such events but it was not a frequent scene for me. At different times of my life I was reawakened to the purpose of my existence but now the time had come to explore how it could happen. Evaluating my life and experiences allowed me to gain a more complete understanding of His power. His grace and mercy became more apparent to me during this time. I knew had it not been for the grace of God the path I had chosen for myself would have been a lot different. God's hand in my life positioned me where I needed and wanted to be. It was this acknowledgment compelling me to seek His presence daily. To thank Him for being present always even if I failed to keep Him first.

It was in college when I first began writing with intentionality. Writing in regard to individual experiences with the intent to motivate others. I was not one hundred percent committed to it. I would write when I felt the desire but would go months without writing. The lack of knowing my purpose specifically was a barrier. Maybe I needed to change my focus from motivating others and knowing-it-all to being led by God. If what was laid on my heart motivated others in the process, so be it. I will admit there were certain things keeping me side-tracked. I like to think the motivation at the time was not strong enough to fully commit. I also was a student-athlete, dedicating most of my time to myself, school, and athletics. A bit self-centered because guys did occupy my time too.

Every year the desire continued to be present, intensifying with time. I knew I had a greater purpose then I was currently living but I had no idea how it would ever come to pass which is why I continued to do my own thing. I did not think I had the means to present the ideas to gain the support to complete the journey so why dedicate too much time to the *what if.*

It takes more than yourself to reach and obtain a goal. To think otherwise would be foolish. But it must be noted, with God taking precedence, He will lead people to you whose role is in stoking the fire. He sent quite a bit of those to redirect some of my decisions. As I look back and even now I see all those people who kept the fire blazing inside whether they knew it or not. I thank those people as they helped see His plans through. It was closer to the end of my time in college when I promised myself I would not let this desire burn out entirely, no matter how long it took to see it come to fruition.

It was time for me to make God proud. For Him to know I was ready to actively seek and live out the purpose in me. At this point I conveyed my strong desire for Him to take the lead so I could follow His footsteps. It was time to put action behind the desire. No longer was my intent about others. My intention was to follow His lead and by doing so those attracted to what was being done would be the souls God intended for me to draw nearer Him. It became solely about Him and less about me (which is still a process). Once I put action behind my love for Him I began to receive on levels unimaginable. Not necessarily in the monetary sense but on a spiritual and emotional level He provided what cannot be given by any other. A peace passing all understanding and joy uncontainable.

Had God not kept me in remembrance of the gift He had put inside of me year after year I would not be writing this now. The spark was ignited but I had to keep the flame going and God in his graciousness would send others to provide a boost. Whether an encouraging conversation with a friend, a motivational word from a livestream broadcast, or a random confirming quote I came across scrolling Pinterest. God has a way of stirring your gift because He knows the glory attached to it.

Now please note, although God was sending blessings of encouragement, the enemy also was sending distractions because he knew what God was up to. Whether it was a person or another mechanism there were definite moments where the enemy had me sidetracked. The enemy does this because he too knows the amount of lives tied to us and he will do all in this power to stop our obedience. This is why it is so important to be active. Actively strengthening our relationship with God. Actively in the Word. Actively feeding our faith. Actively engaged in fruitful associations. Actively involved in spiritually uplifting events. Actively living out our belief. Active in our confidence in Him. We have to understand, God is actively working behind the scenes on our behalf. We serve an active God. Therefore, we must be in active pursuit of what He has called us to do. Once we are in alignment with Him, fully reliant on Him, we will be promoted.

4.

ELEVATE YOUR THOUGHTS

The levels will take you higher while demanding elevation from your previous state of mind.

The staircase set before you is designed to take you up. Do not be overwhelmed by the incline it only implies God wants to take you higher. When called by God, He creates in you an internal yearning. Not only for Him but for the potential of you. It is this desire existent within you constantly demanding your attention. Indicative of your strength to face all the possibilities of your future. Do not be intimidated by the magnitude of your calling, embrace the yearning by acting upon it.

Remember: ***You are much stronger than you think you are and you can do more than what you think you can do.*** To accept Christ into your life you are expanding your abilities because with Him you are not limited you are limitless.

> *I can do all things through Christ who strengthens me. Philippians 4:13*

You can maintain the demands of your purpose if only you demonstrate an earnestness to do so. Do not underestimate you, the people around you, or the strength within you. Utilize your resources. To consult with others is to increase your own understanding. This understanding is part of a learning process necessary to acquire wisdom. Although you can gain wisdom from God, He does not limit your understanding to Him alone.

> *A wise man will hear and increase learning, and a man of understanding will attain wise counsel, to understand a proverb and*

> *an enigma, the words of the wise and their*
> *riddles. The fear of the Lord is the beginning*
> *of knowledge, but fools despise wisdom and*
> *instruction. Proverbs 1:5-7*

A few character traits are given as an indicator of wisdom and understanding. If you believe yourself to be wise you will *hear* and *learn*. If you are a person of understanding you will *attain wise counsel*; others you can look to for further understanding and interpretation. But, it goes on to say *fools despise wisdom and instruction*. It is never the aim to be a fool although I am convinced we all have been one at one point or another. The goal would be to improve upon the skill of a renewed mind. To be open to wisdom and instruction does not necessarily mean you need to apply it immediately. But possess a willingness to listen to understand not simply to respond. Understanding will expand your ability to learn more, acquire wisdom, and evolve. Only fools refuse such things. Fools get too comfortable where they are, sacrificing where they could go. Believe me I have been a fool before. Staying in environments I should not be in, around folks I should not entertain, doing things I do not agree with. Mostly because it yielded temporary pleasure but temporary is the key word. Due to my acquired wisdom and that of others I learned to refuse to stay in a foolish state of mind. Refusing to settle into a place of stagnancy when God was calling me out into a broad place.

*He delivered me from my strong enemy,
from those who hated me, for they were
too strong for me. They confronted me in
the day of my calamity, but the Lord was
my support. He also brought me out into a
broad place; He delivered me because He
delighted in me. Psalm 18: 17-19*

The enemy is actively seeking to consume. To use us up, mentally, physically, emotionally, and spiritually. Yet, Our God is present to be our source of comfort and support. He is rooting for us. He knows the promises granted to us and He backs us up along the way. He brings us out of what we were in. He shows His mercy upon us through deliverance because He *delights* in us. He finds pleasure in His creation; our very lives. This is encouragement for me to press on. To push past people, places, and things not in alignment with His plan.

There have been moments in my past where I have settled. I have found a place of predictability and laid there. I knew what to expect I knew how things were going to go and I was content. It is not always good to be content, at least not always. Think for a moment of being in bed. If you are comfortable you are less likely to get up. You will not move unless you have something to do requiring you to leave what is comfortable to tend to something more important. But when you are uncomfortable in any position you will do more to move to a more desired position. You can only be comfortable or uncomfortable in one position for so long before you start feeling cramped in the limited parameters of your environment. The Lord will do all in His power to ensure you do not stay in bed all your life. You have to explore beyond one position. You have to step out in faith because to be stagnant in any one position is to sacrifice your potential to maximize your abilities.

Essentially, you have to reject inactivity. God is mobile therefore you should be too. There will be challenges but where you may have limitations God has none. How foolish it would be to place restrictions on Him who is able to surpass all of our expectations. We must incline our mind to think more bountifully so we can align ourselves with the abundance of our purpose. To surrender our own ideas is to move a step closer to the potentials of our being. There were times where what once felt comfortable began to feel cramped. Relationships which once felt life-long began to feel uncertain. Decisions that once brought rewards were not reaping the same benefits.

With progression, we have to be willing to adhere to the new demand. The new command, to reach people and make a lasting impact without being hindered by where we once were. We have to be capable of growth. Seeking out what is good for our souls and the souls of others. It may be a tough decision but the decision should always be made for the greater good. With elevation, there must be an adaptation in perspective to focus on what is good.

Finally, brethren, whatever things are true, whatever things are noble, whatever things are just, whatever things are pure, whatever

> *things are lovely, whatever things are of good*
> *report, if there is any virtue and if there is*
> *anything praiseworthy — mediate on these*
> *things. Philippians 4:8*

Shift your focus to advance your progress by dwelling on the positive, departing from the negative, and growing from it all. The victories and losses serve a purpose. Failure allows you to stretch a little more, open your mind a bit more, strengthen your inner self, and come out stronger than before. What you have to understand is every single thing you have been through has been intentional. Serving as either a lesson or a blessing. ***Do not allow temporary defeat to break you, it is meant to build you.*** God would never put you in a position to watch you fail miserably. He may put you in a situation where you are challenged all so you will put your trust in Him. But He believes in you far more than you believe in you. Offering you strength to overcome because He knows you underrate your own abilities.

As frustrating as it is to see children of God undervaluing their immense value we are constantly reminded of our worth through His word. It is available to us to dive into and develop our faith. There is a word in the scripture for you providing the comfort, peace, encouragement (and so on) that you need. There is a word for every season whether happy or sad. When we get active in the word our faith will be reinforced when we apply it to our lives in overcoming obstacles and encouraging our sisters and brothers. We were built to sustain the load; we only have to believe it by walking in our faith.

> *Your sandals shall be iron and bronze;*
> *As your days, so shall your strength be.*
> *Deuteronomy 33:25*

No matter what your day brings you have already been equipped with the strength to bear it. The tenacity to endure it. Life brings with it ups and downs. However, it is up to you to believe no matter what you face you will be blessed by it. Maybe not today or next month but it will work together for your good. You will grow from the experience and if you do not have room to sprout you should be motivated to step out from where you are. Even if uncomfortable. In fact, with discomfort there is an expansion of knowledge which God is always intending to afford you. Look at every challenge, obstacle, barrier, or test as a mechanism to strengthen your character, mind, body, and spirit. You are strong enough, you have to believe you are strong enough. Others will follow your lead because of the strength you exude. Do not be afraid to step into a broader place, beyond where you once were, into where you are called to be.

—

I had been comfortable where I was for too long. Away at college my freshman year I would get homesick. I would miss being in a place of comfort, a place of familiarity. Living in a small city and knowing everyone or at least knowing of everyone and moving to a much bigger city where the comforts of a small place were not present, I would go home often. By often I mean like every weekend. I had a car which I could not drive (a stick shift just made life more difficult) but my mom would pick me up on a Friday after track practice and bring me back Monday before class. This was not just down the road either. I was a good hour and a half away from where I called home (which isn't too far but it was far enough). I purposefully would schedule my class for later in the afternoon or not schedule classes at all on Mondays so I could stay in my place of comfort for as long as possible.

After freshmen year, after being uncomfortable for a year, I realized being uncomfortable is not a bad thing. I began to be okay and satisfied where I was. Okay with the environment and people in it. I was not calling and begging my mom to pick me up every weekend (which she would do) because I felt at peace with where God was taking me. God was giving me revelation. I was beginning to see the blessing of discomfort. Of stepping out in faith, of being in a new place, of experiencing life at a new age, at a time of growth, and trusting the process.

In college, I was exposed to so many new people, from so many different places, and so many unique backgrounds. This helped me to open up my mind. To lift my boundaries and expand my scope of understanding. It was no longer necessary for me to be comfortable, I only wanted to progress. Embracing the people around me. Building lasting relationships with a few great friends.

Working to maximize where I was to become a better me. I began to feed my spirit. Really taking the time to get to know myself, my motivations, my aspirations.

Listening to pastors preach and teach the word, especially on Sunday. I did not attend church in the city I went to college so I resorted to other means like online preachers and visiting area churches with friends. Attending campus sponsored events: sporting events (baseball games were a favorite), comedy shows, fashion shows, Greek life events, concerts, motivational speaking events (Eric Thomas had to be another favorite), political events (Barack Obama was yet another favorite). Pretty much all the free events (we are talking about college kids here, free was our love language). Talking with peers and teammates for hours who shared similar desires to reach new heights or learn new things. Occasionally, showing up to evening bible study (I was not as committed as I should have been).

Most of it was beneficial. Some things left me inspired. Other things gave me more clarity as to why I do what I do because of who I represent. I began to understand the importance of your environment and the people you surround yourself with. The importance of what and who you embrace. I know it is not always something within your control, especially at a young age, but know you do not have to stay in an environment of predictability. By doing so you could be missing out on opportunities to grow, expand your parameters and step closer to your purpose.

I knew if I was going to accomplish anything I had to

feed my spirit which in turn stimulated my desires to fulfill my purpose. This was not all for my own gain. Reciprocity is something I strongly believe in so it was involved too. Whether it was offering advice, sowing into a ministry, or expressing gratitude to others. I did nothing out of spite but everything with intent and purpose. Understanding, I needed to become intentional with my time. Actively pursuing opportunities to grow. Making the most out of where I was physically in order to progress and improve upon myself spiritually and mentally. I had to put in the effort and it was then when true growth began. All of that had taken place after my first couple years of college. I say after my first couple years because the first two were a lot of trial and error. Making mistakes, learning from them, making more mistakes, learning from them. It was my goal not to make the same mistake twice (as I said before) so at least I was learning from them and not repeating them. I am an avid believer that everything happens for a reason and I know my not-so-good choices led me to make better choices. Life's processes are great teachers and it is up to us to learn the lessons and apply what we have learned. That is what I was beginning to do.

IT'S ALL ABOUT ACTION

5.

BELIEVE IT TO ACHIEVE IT

Faith is the substance of things hoped for, the evidence of things not seen but you better believe they are coming.

Faith appeals to the senses. Not in the literal sense but the spiritual sense (at times in the literal sense). It is being moved in a way where you hear from God, sense His presence, and see in a whole new realm.

It activates the mind into accepting the notion of hope with an expectation to access what is hoped for. Faith is the trigger expelling doses of ambition. The string you engage to pull back the arrow. Letting it go once you have acquired enough resistance to propel it forward, right on target. With it you can obtain that which you are inclined to achieve, without it what you have been predestined for becomes dormant. You have to remain faithful in your pursuit regardless of the time it takes to see it come to pass. You have to believe in God, His process, and His timing. Believe He is who He says He is and He can do what He says He can do. Have faith in the one who is always faithful.

> *But without faith it is impossible to please Him, for he who comes to God must believe that He is, and that he is a rewarder of those who diligently seek Him. Hebrews 11:6*

Faith is the requirement for endless possibilities and trust will allow you to reach your potential. You will be rewarded for your diligence in seeking Him as long as you have faith in Him. You have to align yourself with God. Be on one accord with Him. In working order with the Lord. When the faith test is presented it is up to you to pass or fail. Do not look at the action you have to put in and give up. Thank God for His belief in you, your capabilities, and pursue. Apply yourself. If He has put you to the test it is with good intention, knowing you are able, by faith, to pass. ***When we question our abilities, essentially, we question His.*** There are many things I am unable to do alone, however, with Him, I can do all things. Because I have faith to believe this, I therefore, can do all things.

What is upsetting is when we lack the faith to do what He knows we can do. It is upsetting because when you read the Bible and understand the words you read, to question Him illustrates your unbelief in Him. Your unbelief in Him expresses your lack of faith. We know without faith we cannot please Him and in a world of chaos we need to believe. Believe He is Our Source for whatever it is we need. We need to hope for things and believe we can achieve them. We need His power to be present on earth as it is in heaven. Our prayers should reflect our need for His presence. We should show no anxiety when it comes to God. There should be no reservations held toward who He is, what He can do, and what we can do because He lives in us. We may question but we must not let it stop us from asking and believing.

> *Be anxious for nothing, but in everything by prayer and supplication, with thanksgiving, let your requests be made known to God;*
> *Philippians 4:6*

He not only knows what we are capable of but He

knows what He is capable of (which is all things). So, when we sell ourselves short we are demonstrating distrust. Yet, His desire is for us to ask of Him what we want to ask without doubting. He wants us to ask humbly, with gratitude. He wants us to pray diligently as our prayers are preparation for advancement. But still, we lack faith. We deprive Him of the ability to bless us. God wants to bless us. He is not the one who stops a blessing or holds out on a blessing or blocks a blessing, we do. We do it because we lack commitment. We are not fully dedicated. We do not fully trust in God because if we did these things *it*, whatever *it* is, would come to pass.

> *Commit your way to the Lord, trust also in Him, and he shall bring it to pass. Psalms 37:5*

Many of us are willing to commit to Him but not fully. Myself included. This is why certain things are not happening in the way or in the time we thought they should. We are not where we thought we would be because we are one foot in and one foot out. God is not fond of us when we are not all in (Revelation 3:16). We straddle the fence so we have an excuse for why we failed but we are missing the fundamental piece. We must have faith *and* works. Not faith alone. Faith works with our works but if we expect faith to do the work we are mistaken.

> *For as the body without the spirit is dead, so faith without works is dead also. James 2:26*

The hurdle in front of you will not simply disappear due to your faith. However, with your faith *and* your works you possess the ability to overcome it. I myself am not the biggest fan of hurdles whether a physical hurdle (popular in track & field) or life's hurdles but I have a reason. I do not like them, the physical or the literal, because they have knocked me to the ground a number of times, leaving a lasting impression. What is even more interesting about the physical hurdle knocking me down is I never participated in hurdles in a meet. Sprinting alone was enough of a challenge and jumping far (long, not high) was always what I enjoyed, however, to do them well and develop skill and precision required hurdle drills during practice (sigh). I did not particularly like the hurdle drills but the beauty of eventually overcoming the hurdle both physically and mentally brought me peace *but* the peace definitely did not come until *after* the leap. Peace came after clearing the barrier without being knocked to the ground but first I had to overcome the mental barrier to overcome the physical barrier. I could not have overcome either one without faith *and* works.

The process of persistence is taking on an obstacle time and time again until it becomes a stepping stone. Doing so, reinforces the level of belief and effort it takes to accomplish it. It is challenging. We want to be able to do all things but at times we neglect to trust Him for it because it is difficult. We want the process to be easy. Why have to work too hard for anything or activate any level of faith? Yes, what appears to be an overnight success is alluring but trust me, it was not an overnight success. We are lazy to think true success can be obtained in 24 hours alone. No, it takes many of those 24 hours to accomplish goals but when things do not go our way we immediately look for an excuse. We look to blame someone else for why we gave up. Questioning how we ended up in this position and justifying why we could not get over the hurdle. When ultimately, we decide.

We decide whether to believe in God or not. Whether to trust Him or not. We decide whether to value ourselves or not. Every morning we make the decision to better our life or someone else's. We decide what kind of day we are going to have. Whether we are going to rise to the occasion or shrink back in fear. We have the power to exemplify the life we want to live but it is not going to be easy. God did not promise ease. The hard days are meant to make us stronger and better equipped. We have to decide to accept God as our guide and walk in our purpose. Over obstacles, through them, but not around them. Fighting the good fight of faith. Putting effort into it. We have a divine purpose to fulfill and maneuvering through each phase will accelerate us to new levels. They say new levels, new devils. In essence, He is continually prepping us for what is still to come while expanding our territory as we progress.

We can move forward if we put our trust in the right place, in Him. He has our best interest in mind. There have been times when we lend more trust to others who fail us time and time again. Why do we give them so much authority in our lives? Why not put our trust in God who is working all things together for our good? By trusting Him we will receive indicators of what is ours to possess. Our paths will be made straighter, leading us to what was already ours. Trusting is what will prompt us to go possess what has our name on it. We may not see it physically (yet) but we have to trust with such fervency that it can happen because this intensity will provoke us to go and get it.

> *Trust in the Lord with all your heart, and lean not on your own understanding; in all your ways acknowledge Him, and he shall direct your paths. Proverbs 3:5-6*

Just because you do not have it yet does not imply it is not already yours. Look to God and He will show you. If you know what is yours then it becomes your duty to go get what belongs to you. ***Faith fuels your desire and action goes and gets it.*** You need both to attain what God has for you. He is a dispenser of opportunities. He dispenses it but you have to grab it. You have to have enough faith to put the quarter in, knowing He will give you something as a reward for your faith. You only need to act upon it and ready yourself to seize it. Do not get frustrated when the machine takes your quarter with no return. You will not always get a blessing when you want it. It could be, what you wanted was never a blessing to begin with but a curse and you have not received it because He was sparring you from it. Be patient, the next attempt may yield greater returns. Two is better than one.

I lost numerous dollars and quarters from those

machines enticing me to play for a chance at a prize. The excitement was always the greatest when the stuffed animal was hanging over the ledge but just not enough to fall. In the midst of trying again, and again, when the claw grabbed hold of another prize, it would just so happen to knock the intended one down the trapped door with it; two for one, score. Sometimes you will have to try again because your initial approach was not effective. Typically, your second go around is easier than before because you know what to expect and are better equipped to handle what you know is to come. If you do not receive it, consider you may not be prepared for it. This was an eye-opening revelation for me to recognize I may be the one delaying my blessing because I may not be ready to receive it. I still am preparing myself to receive blessings I have prayed for but the preparation is time well spent. I look at each day I am granted as an opportunity to live in His fullness.

> *Blessed be the Lord, who daily loads us with*
> *benefits, the God of our salvation. Selah.*
> *Psalm 68:19*

Continually God provides us with assets to encourage our prosperity. He thinks and acts on a much broader scale. He sees what we do not see. He knows what is on the inside. He has planted a seed in us with an expectation of what He knows can happen. It is up to us to believe in His power and His ways. He gives chance after chance and opportunity after opportunity for us to activate our faith in Him. He wants us to live out our faith by walking the walk with Him.

We have to put in the effort to allow our faith to control our actions. We cannot halfway believe in God. Our actions have to match our faith. If we believe in His word we have to implement aspects of our consumption of the word into our lives. Will we be perfect? Not exactly, but we will become better people. You see anyone can talk about the word and not apply it to their life. I see it all the time. I use to do the same thing. In order to move to the next level and live the life God has planned for us we have to do and we have to prepare for where He is leading us every opportunity we get. The seasons when we feel as if nothing is happening is the season we should be preparing the most. In this preparation ensure you are in relationship with Him. First by believing, then solidifying your belief by action. Being in relationship with Him is certainly the foundation, it is also something you will be working to strengthen day by day. In conjunction with this, continue preparing yourself by reading the word, connecting with like-minded peers, furthering your knowledge, increasing your wisdom, creating, crafting, writing, reading, studying, and sharing. Embrace your current season but anticipate the next through prayer and preparation so you are ready when it comes.

—

Action can be the most difficult task for people. I was among them, the sitters, who would sit, expecting things to happen without putting in any great amount of effort. I would do but it would be the bare minimum, in regard to my purpose. I thought if I worked on it, even sporadically, things would begin to manifest. Soon I realized you only see progress in an area in which you dedicate an ample amount of your attention. If you dedicate a little bit of time you get a little bit in return.

Once I considered the thought I could see this very notion reflected in different aspects of my life. The relationships I worked to improve and inspire growth were thriving and those neglected began to fade. Studying weeks in advance for a test yielded satisfactory grades but last-minute preparation left me displeased. A focused mindset at practice delivered great outcomes during the competition but a distracted mind led to poor performances. After much thought, I realized it is not only attention (because that can be misused) but more specifically a choice to commit entirely to obtaining what you desire. When everything in you is dedicated to achieve that which you seek. When your mind, body, and spirit is on the same page and moving in the same direction.

It was not until I committed to writing that the process itself became easier. Not to say there are not days where I am uninspired to write because there are. But when I am intentional, setting aside time devoted specifically to either me, my laptop, and Microsoft Word, or me and a pen and paper the words begin to flow.

I recognized envisioning where you want to go is just as important as going. So, I started to go on the things I previously had stopped, kicked back, and relaxed by. Like in this very moment. I have been working on this book for years. But just recently I committed thirty minutes to an hour of my days, editing. Most times, the timer would buzz and I would think to myself "yes, I had reached the requirement" but words would continue to rush out and I would let them. What I committed thirty minutes or an hour to would turn into nearly two hours of creative flow. I sacrificed idle time to put this book in your hands because I understand there are souls to save and lives to change. My hours of watching TV or scrolling through Instagram are not making the impact I know I am intended for. Disclaimer: I do enjoy Instagram but can take time away when necessary. You certainly should take time away from anything unproductive to your growth. If you are spending hours on end on social media you may need to take a break. I have done so numerous times and it is always nice to decompress, reprioritize, and move onward. It could be simply deleting the app off your phone for a day, or two, or three. It is totally up to you. I am only recommending what I have done because it has worked for me. It has allowed me to dive deeper into the word of God. It has allowed me to strengthen the bond I share with Him. It has allowed me to share precious moments with my nieces and nephews, face-to-face, hearing their stories and seeing their excitement. It has allowed me to connect with others. It has allowed me to write, read, create. It has allowed me the opportunity to take in the beauty around me. To see, hear, and smell all the Creator has designed for us.

In this time of silenced distractions really begin to focus on what is important to you. Once I knew writing was something tied to a greater purpose for me I began to pray God would have His way in this. If it was meant to impact the lives of others I put it in God's hands but I did not stop there. Not because I did not trust God but because God was not going to write the book for me. He sent me to write the book. He put those thoughts, experiences, desires in my heart to equip, prepare, and prompt me to do the writing. So, writing is what I intended to do. Write until the words stopped making sense (because the editing would address this). To attend writing workshops. Connect with authors. Read books written by author's who inspired me. It is still a dream of mine to get paid to read books all day. I am going to back up a second to say, vision is important. It is important to what you imagine and understand. Giving you a perspective from which to see your vision through to completion. This is all significant. It sets the pace but without action it rarely goes anywhere.

This book would not be in your hands right now if it were not for me acting on the words consuming my thoughts and being strategic about the way they come together. To accomplish this I had to write, write, and write some more. I had to edit, read, erase, and rewrite. I had to reach out to people who take the words I have written, like the way I have written them, see the potential of them, and agree to edit, rework, and edit some more. By the time it gets in front of you it is an immaculate work (at least I like to think so). There is a lot of work involved. A lot of time. A lot of effort. A lot of sacrifice. A lot of prayer. A lot of defeat. But do not let *a lot* stop your pursuit.

There is a reason why you are doing what you are doing. Even if it is unknown right now, let it drive you to wake up a bit earlier and stay up a bit later. To motivate you in the moments of rejection to try again. Let it consume a portion of your 24 hours, even if only 30 minutes. You have to invest if you want to see a return. It was not until I began committing more of my time and energy to writing that I could see it flourishing. Before I set aside the time it sat dormant. The good fruit within me could not prosper until I tended to it often. I could no longer give it some time here and there. I had to get in the habit of writing, daily. The dedication then allowed me to see how the good fruit was expanding, consuming more areas of my life, and yielding returns. I decided to invest in what I felt led to do. Boy, did that decision require a lot of time and energy. But, it was so worth every bit of it. To give of myself in order to live in alignment with my purpose is a gift that continues to give. All because I acted on the decision instead of expecting the decision to act on itself.

6.

Actions speak loudest

When you become less impressed by words let your actions speak.

Never forget the power of action. Words can make actions seem easy but actions do not always come easy. In our faith walk we have to walk through some things and talk through some things. They say "easier said than done" because to speak a thing requires far less energy than to do it.

Effort is necessary if you intend to reach any goal you set for yourself and anything worth having or doing requires it. What you speak into the atmosphere can only come to pass if there is a force and a strong work ethic, pushing it into existence.

> *Therefore, my beloved brethren, be steadfast,*
> *immovable, always abounding in the work*
> *of the Lord, knowing that your labor is not*
> *in vain in the Lord. 1 Corinthians 15:58*

For the scripture to say, *know* that *your labor* is *not* in *vain* indicates the work is necessary. It is not all for nothing. It will serve a purpose.

You alone are a force to be reckoned with if only you apply yourself. The power within you is a source of your strength. What you say can only take you so far. What you do will take you the rest of the way. Not because words are meaningless they just mean less until they are backed by action.

We tend to lose sight of the importance of not only saying but doing what reflects our own sincerity. To be able to express our self in ways beyond our words reaffirms our level of commitment.

If you are not committed to what you are speaking it becomes difficult for others to believe in you and the places you intend to go require others to be on board. You do not need many but you need enough. Jesus had 12. Even in that small number there was betrayal, back-stabbers, and liars. But there were also mortars, lovers, and servants. When building your team, it is imperative to choose wisely and even in your choosing you may make a mistake or two but do not allow that to stop you from doing what the Lord has led you to do.

> *For where two or three are gathered together in my name, I am there in the midst of them. Matthew 18:20*

His intention for us is to engage with others, at least someone (other than ourselves). He has designed us in working order among others which is why our team should be cohesive.

If the bond is not concrete, you may want to consider looking elsewhere because you want a secure framework. If your foundation is not solid it will likely fall. In the beginning, the exterior may match the house of your dreams but it is deeper than surface level. It is not just about looks, it is about whether it can sustain growth. Ask yourself (and God):

1. No matter the duration, can the weight of the load be maintained?

2. Can others be added to the equation without being limited in parameter?

3. Can it weather the storm?

A home may seem like a great fit but over time things may start to fall apart.

Like a house with a shaky foundation, with time you start to see the cracks and leaks. You hear the creaks. It can be repaired but you have to gut it out. Get rid of some things. Rip up the old gunk obscuring your view. You have to go all the way down to the foundation, the studs, the framework, the core, and figure out what it was built on in order to see what it can be. ***If you want to see the potential of something, you have to know its foundation.*** Find out what it was made to do. Understand the reactions and functions. Once you see the punctures and stains you can see what kind of work you will need to put in to fix the issue.

We are moving beyond the structure of a home and considering the structure of a person. Determining whether a relationship will be of great benefit after digging to the core. Seeing a person beyond their outer appearances.

Just make sure you know who you are working with. We could all benefit from some renovation. The efforts of each person involved should indicate some resemblance. Everyone has something to offer in the restoration process. If we are on the same team we should share similar passions of winning and prospering together. My absence should not compromise workmanship, effort, or efficiency. What is required should be done at a high standard. We should be able to count on each other to match our efforts regardless of position and this is true whether in personal relationships or business.

> *Two are better than one, because they have a good reward for their labor. For if they fall, one will lift up his companion. But woe to him who is alone when he falls, for he has no one to help him up. Ecclesiastes 4:9-10*

You should be surrounded with people who will lift you up. People who will put in the effort to build and ensure completion. Establish standards of operation to evaluate the effort of the paddlers on your boat. If you are not rowing with me we are not going anywhere. What benefit is it to go around in circles? Circling the same thing, the same mountain, the same sin over and over again?

Progress requires onward motion. If you cannot meet the needs we will have to reevaluate your position. If you want to sit lazily maybe you are better off on land. On the boat, you have to work. On the boat, you have to put an ample amount of effort into moving from one point to the next point and so on. When we get to our destination we can relax (temporarily). It is a period of time to recuperate and rejuvenate the body to better supply the demand.

Everyone on board must know they are valuable to the carrying out of the mission. Note: the reward can be anything. Happiness, good health, financial stability, a significant other, peace, understanding; the rewards are endless. If those on your team place an equal or greater amount of effort into the task at hand everyone benefits. If I am growing you are growing too.

> *As iron sharpens iron, so a man sharpens the*
> *countenance of his friend. Proverbs 27:17*

Do not limit the scope of your abilities. The blessing of your presence should benefit more than yourself. You are capable of improving the lives of others and vice versa if you apply and share the gifts you have been given. You can affect more than just you, or your spouse, or your family, or your friends. You can affect neighbors, strangers, different communities, and even countries.

There comes a point where you have to say, I only want to make you better and I suspect you expect the same from me. You have to put it on the table to know whether you are in alignment with one another. By being on one accord there is nothing the two of you or three of you, or four, or five cannot accomplish. A united front serves as an advantage because everyone is pushing towards one goal with different skills to offer.

There is power in unity and whenever God is present there is ample opportunity. In every aspect of your life work with God. You have to include Him in the process. He should be your CEO. The one you refer to, humbly, before you make your next move. This allows you to make the right move by following His lead instead of your own. If you are linked with Him you are in good company. But, He wants you to associate and unite with others who can also provide a voice of reason, a wise suggestion, a listening ear.

He wants us to be interconnected, touching one another with the love, power, and wisdom bestowed in us by Him. We cannot do this alone. I repeat. We cannot do this alone. Certainly not without Him. And we make it more difficult when we refuse to include others in the process. To get to the places we want to go and reach the folks intended to reach we have to be able to relate to more than ourselves. We have to be able to connect with more than just the person looking back at us in the mirror. Will there be moments of heartache, loneliness, and disappointment? Yes. Naysayers, backstabbers, and liars? Absolutely. But also, there will be seasons of joy, togetherness, and peace. People who support, love, and fight for you, not against you.

On this journey, progressing from one season to the next we must understand the intentionality of it all. It serves a particular purpose. You serve a particular purpose and the people around you serve a purpose too. There will be times when you are filled up and times when you are left empty. Times of achievement and times of growth. If you can look at other's experiences without judgment but with love, you draw nearer to God. Not caving to the acceptance of this world but standing firm in your faith by sharing with others the goodness of the Lord.

Declare His glory among the nations, His wonders among all peoples. Psalm 96:3

Share what He has brought you to and what He has brought you through. Share the triumph and glory of being His and maneuvering through life with Him versus without Him. Share the blessing of His constant presence, through the thick and thin and this or that. Because speaking of all He has been through with you is encouragement for others that He can and will do the same for them. It takes all of that. The highs and lows. Joys and sorrows. To see your progress and His presence through it all.

—

I had to evaluate what or who I was committing my attention to and whether the commitment was mutually beneficial. I did not want to waste precious energy on anything not propelling me toward my destiny. Also, I wanted to demonstrate to God, His preeminence. No one had more of my attention than Him. At times feeling guilty when I put others before Him (including family). There were seasons of my life when others had more of my attention than Him but I continually reevaluate priority level. Once I decided to allow Him to reign others took the backseat or were kicked out of the car altogether. Through my actions, I was showing Him what I deemed to be important.

I began to structure my life with Him as the focal point. Reminding myself not to be discouraged when I put Him first and my "friends" fell to the way side, stopped calling, texting or the connection was lost. Unfortunately, or fortunately not everyone we once knew will move forward with us in this process of progression. If I am not progressing with you I would hate to be the reason you were not progressing so in efforts to increase functionality something or someone needs to go. I was okay with the departure because the focus was no longer about someone it was about The One. Making sure relationships were for His glory and not in conflict with His plan. Shedding His light into their lives even if the connection faded.

I began to dedicate the first part of my morning to reading a bible verse, saying a prayer, and thanking Him. We have become a poorly mannered society with not enough people in the world thanking Him for all He is or does or will do. If proper manners were not instilled in you growing up it would be appropriate to develop those habits now. I made it my duty (and still do) to express my gratitude. I thank Him for everything. For little things and big things. I thank Him for life, for eyes to see, and ears to hear. I thank Him for mobility and good health. I thank Him for things often taken for granted. I thank Him for peace. I thank Him for allowing me another day to be on earth to work toward fulfilling the purpose within me. I thank Him for the people He has led into and out of my life for my good. I thank Him for His constant presence; something I would be completely lost without. I thank Him for grace and mercy as it has sustained me.

It is common for us to forget the importance of conveying our thanks to those we appreciate. Often, we get so caught up in our daily lives we fail to express how much we care for those present in our lives. Unfortunately, for some the time will never come again to verbalize such things. This makes the gesture much more significant. Understanding this I knew I had to begin showing God how much I appreciated (beyond words) His presence in my life and His overflow of blessings (in whatever form).

Each day it is important for me and you too, to not only express with words but through action our gratitude. Little things can be done as an act of thanks. I could not let another day go by without dedicating intentional time to my purpose. I worked. I wrote. I read. I utilized every ounce of energy toward improving myself. Every opportunity given to invest in my future I intended to take. I wanted to let others know of my appreciation of their commitment too. I sent heartfelt cards that I actually took the time to write personalized messages in. I bought random gifts. I sent encouraging texts. Small efforts to demonstrate my thanks but much more important than material things, I spent time, an invaluable gift of presence.

There is no greater gift than being present. I understand you cannot be present in every relationship twenty-four hours a day, seven days a week because there are certain demands required from you but some time should be spent loving (it is what we were sent here to do). It was time to assess priority, value, and position. I had to begin to sacrifice relationships, environments, and some of my own selfish desires for His plans. It was time to fulfill my purpose so I could touch lives. It was time to show those I love what I had been working toward. I had to cut down slack time instead of watching television or tending to social media or other leisure activities for hours I inclined myself to watering, plucking, and cultivating the seed of purpose placed in me so it could continuously grow. Not that I no longer continued to use these things but I began to put time limits on my use. Setting boundaries for myself to better utilize my 24 hours.

I had to fertilize the seeds and pull the weeds which takes time. The process of plucking was strenuous in itself especially when things had taken root. But even more important was watering and feeding what was feeding me. What was pouring itself into me needed to be replenished. It was time for me to invest back into what was investing in me. Allowing the light beaming within me to shine through me into others and through them. ***Relationships can either sustain you or drain you.*** It was my prerogative to build upon what was sustaining me, speaking life into me, and fueling the fire inside while I reciprocated by doing the same for them, for Him. This was no overnight process. This was years of drawing close to God, pulling away from Him, seeking forgiveness, and recommitting to His purposes, plans, and people.

THE TIME IS ALWAYS NOW

7.

BALANCE THE IMBALANCE

You cannot be selfish and sacrificial at the same time so choose wisely.

Sacrificing is part of progressing. The intent is to maximize your walk with God. Surrendering your plan for His own. Sacrificing your will for His.

Most of us have been afraid to sacrifice our control (what little bit we have). Afraid to let Him take the lead in this dance although He has already mastered the steps. Being of this world we allow the reality of a situation, what we see with our natural eye, to control our movements. Rather than relying on the capabilities of Our Orchestrator to work all things together for good to them that Love Him, to them who are called according to His purpose (Romans 8:28).

This definition of Orchestrator stood out to me:

> to arrange or manipulate, especially by means of clever or thorough planning or maneuvering: to orchestrate a profitable trade agreement. (dictionary.com)

He is working out the intricacies and complexities for our benefit. He wants our works to be profitable, our works, in exchange for His blessings. ***Reciprocity and sacrifice are two ingredients to a healthy relationship.***

How we respond to the exchange, the demand to our supply, is a demonstration of our faith. To remain faithful no matter the circumstance is an illustration of our inner strength, along with how much we truly trust His plan for our lives. Whatever you go through it is not meant to take you out, it is meant to take you up. To build you up in terms of strength, lift you if you have fallen, and elevate you to new realms of opportunity.

Repeatedly in the word we are informed of the strength and power in us. If only we activate our faith to trigger our strength. We are given power and it stays dormant if it is not accessed. It is time to demonstrate our power over the enemy.

> *Behold, I give you the authority to trample on serpents and scorpions, and over all the power of the enemy, and nothing shall by any means hurt you. Luke 10:19*

You are made of powerful stuff. Nothing can cause you harm, but as much as you hold the power you also withhold it. Some things hurt you but they should not be hurting you.

We have to stop allowing certain things or certain people to hold such authority over us. We have to utilize the power given to us instead of cowering in the corner in fear of the outcome. We must put our power, the power within, on display. It is time to gain security over our insecurities, over our fears, and uncertainties. We have authority over all of it. We cannot fully achieve the blessings of God if we do not fight the good fight of faith. ***It is a fight to be faithful.*** Just as it is a fight to be trusting and courageous.

You are not weak, you are strong and even when you are weak you are strong so you should never be intimidated by trials, these instances are opportunities to increase strength. Your life is a testament to your strength which is really His strength within you and you are much stronger than you realize because of it.

> *Therefore I take pleasure in infirmities, in reproaches, in needs, in persecutions, in distresses, for Christ's sake. For when I am weak, then I am strong. 2 Corinthians 12:10*

Remove the fear of failure from your mind. You only fail when you quit. If you do not quit you will not fail. The strength within you will take you out of a trying situation, it will protect you from the enemy, it will increase your learning, and maximize your potential. You have to get out of the habit of doubting, worrying, and questioning your abilities. When you stop these destructive thoughts, you open the door so all things good and pure can come inside.

> *For the weapons of our warfare are not carnal but mighty in God for pulling down strongholds, casting down arguments and every high thing that exalts itself against the knowledge of God, bringing every thought into captivity to the obedience of Christ, and being ready to punish all disobedience when your obedience is fulfilled. 2 Corinthians 10:4-6*

When you are obedient to God, you are making a

sacrifice. You are refusing to be a source of your own pain. No longer suffering through a situation but standing up to what is trying to tear you down, so that it too will be in obedience to God's Will. He has dominion over all but all is not in obedience to Him. It is time to sacrifice yourself, what you thought was working, the plan you had in mind, in order to withstand the enemy and release Gods power over you.

> *Therefore by Him let us continually offer the sacrifice of praise to God, that is, the fruit of our lips, giving thanks to His name. But do not forget to do good and to share, for with such sacrifices God is well pleased. Hebrews 13:15-16*

Your sacrifice is an expression of your gratitude. You thank God through your praise and your prayers. Your sacrifice then is tied to how you communicate. What you speak can be the difference of a blessing and a curse so you want to be alert to the words exiting your lips. Your words can be as powerful as your actions so do not limit the good you can do to only your actions. What you say can have a lasting impact as well. The book of God is composed of words which resonate with people generation after generation yet His actions were of equal importance. What was said and done serve as a depiction of God's love which can be seen through His sacrifices.

> *For God so loved the world that He gave His only begotten Son, that whoever believes in*

> *Him should not perish but have everlasting*
> *life. John 3:16*

The ultimate sacrifice yet the greatest display of His love. He sacrificed His son knowing the spiritual presence of Christ would be much more beneficial to the world than His physical presence on earth. A display of His unconditional love, despite the pain endured. ***Sometimes it takes pain to receive power.***

What are you willing to sacrifice in order to release the power of God in your life? You can certainly strengthen your relationship with God by dedicating yourself to the purpose He has ordained for you, not the purpose you have ordained for you. If you think you know who or what God has for you and it is not what He had in mind, He is going to make sure you get every ounce of what you thought you wanted out of it. The good and the bad. God has a sense of humor (even if He is the only one laughing). He wants to ensure you learn from your choices. He is the best teacher because He goes over what you did wrong until you get it right. Eventually you understand His way is more suitable to your growing process. His way may have less pain involved than your way. His way may contain less obstacles than your way. His plan for you started as a thought, as an idea, and those thoughts are always well intended.

> *For I know the thoughts that I think toward*
> *you, says the Lord, thoughts of peace and*

> *not of evil, to give you a future and a hope.*
> *Jeremiah 29:11*

Without hope, there is a lack of confidence and without confidence there is a lack of action. You are meant to *hope for* because your desire will entice action. If you hope for something, you are confident enough to believe what you hope for is yours. This hope provides you an opportunity to better not only yourself but others. Self-improvement is great but it is not the only improvement you should seek.

You have to pour into those around you and those who stay around should also be an addition to your wellbeing. Ultimately, be aware of what or who affects your walk with God.

1. Be conscious of the message you send and receive because how you feel and how you make others feel is totally up to you.

2. Do not compromise your happiness based on the opinions of those who are saturated with their own insecurities.

3. Identify the beneficial, continue exposure to such but learn from and remove all other impurities.

Everyone is not entitled to the gifts of you (and I say that humbly). Make sure you do not freely give something that is a privilege to receive. Not all are willing to make the sacrifices you have made and it is necessary to guard yourself. I am not suggesting you hide your gifts but rather I am suggesting the opposite. This book actually encourages you to be transparent. I am simply suggesting you refuse to allow anyone to taint your ideas, beliefs, and desires. Your circle of confidants should be supporting the purpose of you and there is no room for negativity to stay. Now a little tough love or voicing concern even if it is not what you want to hear, is not negative. You need some people in your life who will keep you accountable and level-headed. Simply reduce the influence your haters, doubters, or skeptics have over the direction of your life. What you do has nothing to do with them specifically. It is more so about speaking His goodness, it will reach who it is intended for and make a difference (however big or small).

—

I knew I had to sacrifice what I wanted for what He wanted for me. Soon realizing how much peace I received from such sacrifice. What I had chosen had once been fulfilling but now it left me wanting more. It was not filling me up completely. I knew God not only wanted to fill me up but He wanted to provide overflow. Knowing this, I knew I had to sacrifice some relationships despite their importance to me because they were no longer productive. I had to give up the things providing temporary satisfaction. I had to let go of whatever was wasting too much of my time. God wants to give you more than short-term gratification. He wants you to be efficient and you cannot be efficient if you do not make sacrifices.

I am an advocate for reciprocity and if it is not present in any type of relationship or instance I can no longer be tied up with it. At times, you have to love people from a distance. Take a step back and evaluate the entire situation to figure out if it is worth investing more time and energy into. There are some things you can have a connection to, without being involved with. I may have dated so and so, I may have a connection to them, but I am no longer involved with them. I may have participated in athletics and had a connection to the sport but I am no longer active in the athletic program. I might have been friends with a group of people during a certain period of time, so I have a connection to them but I am no longer a part of the clique. If the clique even exists. Separation may be difficult at first but detachment from things negatively influencing your growth or preventing it is the only way you will continue to grow.

I have never liked giving up on people. It can be a painful process initially but what I have learned is, I am not giving up if I have given all. If a relationship expires the roles have been fulfilled. In the same way you retire from a sport after you have endured to the end. After you have maximized your potential in an area and can offer no more of yourself without being a detriment it is time to go.

God is not a fan of dry places so I had to sacrifice certain environments I was putting myself in because they were dry. They left me thirsty and wanting more.

Do you remember when the Samaritan woman met Jesus at the well? She did not intend to meet Him there, she was drawing water per usual when He struck up conversation.

> *Jesus answered and said to her, "whoever drinks of this water will thirst again, but whoever drinks of the water that I shall give him will never thirst. But the water that I shall give him will become in him a fountain of water springing up into everlasting life."*
> *John 4:13-14*

This woman was a bit scandalous. She was thirsty. She had previously had 5 husbands and the man she was currently with was not her husband. She was in a dry place. Yet when He spoke to her about providing a drink from a place that will quench her thirst, she had to have it. She wanted to be satisfied, completely. Not only in relationships but in different areas of life, she wanted to be completely whole. I can relate. I too desire to be filled up until I overflow. Not drawing satisfaction from things that leave me parched, temporarily filling the void but not permanently sufficient. I had to let some things, places, and people go. Thinking back to what once use to bring me great pleasure now it left me disappointed. Sometimes relationships have to end and environments have to change in order for true growth to take place. I had been investing more time in people and less time in

God. Once I began prioritizing my time appropriately God started to move.

I was in a place I no longer wanted to be. I was there long enough to see it was time to go. You see, you get to a point where you are no longer satisfied with what you used to be satisfied with. You no longer get the same gratification from something you used to get. You no longer fit with the groups of people you used to fit with. You begin to realize the places you used to feel comfortable in no longer grant such comfort and you begin to move. You sacrifice where you were in order to grow into where God is taking you. ***You have to refuse to return to the limited parameters of past pleasures.***

I recognized the more I depended on His guidance the fewer people were around me. It may become a bit isolated on the way to your destiny. I used this time to discover more about me. I fell in love with who I was and who I was becoming. I could manage being alone. I may desire to be in a relationship but I will not settle for one. There are certain qualifications each of us must make. We cannot sacrifice who God called us to be based on who we are with. I have developed a greater appreciation for who God called me to be and I will not quit on myself. I am too determined.

Along the way, the world attempts to distort your perspective by placing doubt on your dreams and aspirations. I remind myself how I may be in this world but I am not of this world (John 17:16). I respect the originality of my being and I am bold enough to believe in me even if the world is against me (and this is a continual effort).

I get caught up in the quality of a person much more now versus the quantity of people I have relationships with. I understand how much of a disservice it would be to stay in relationships with no peace and no prosperity. If you want to remain stagnant in your situation so be it but I refuse to allow the enemy to hold me back from my destiny. I have too much strength in me to be held down. Too much to do to be sitting around. I trust God to lead me but I have to continually strengthen that trust. There were certainly times where I took the lead and things did not exactly end in my favor. The beauty though is, each day is another opportunity to draw closer to Him. Each day is an opportunity to give Him the reigns and completely surrender. By honoring Him, He continues to bless me. The genuine relationships serve as an indicator of His appeasement.

I am a fan of those relationships that can just pick up where they left off without a bit of hesitancy. Those relationships that are filled and flowing with authenticity. Now I enter into environments of peace whereas before I would put myself in environments of sin. I can discern places or people who will negatively impact my mood, thoughts, actions and I distance myself from such things by no longer exposing myself to it. I know my limits and I became okay with declining an invitation to a place I did not want to revisit. By realigning myself with God, He equips me with what I need for the season I am in.

> *No weapon formed against you shall prosper, and every tongue which rises against you in judgment you shall condemn. This is the heritage of the servants of the Lord, and their righteousness is from Me," says the Lord. Isaiah 54:17*

The enemy will come full force but will flee because of the God in me. The weapon will form but it will not be able to prosper. What is said against me will be condemned.

He is for us, has equipped us, and lives within us. He is our balance.

8.

IT'S YOUR TIME NOW

Alyssa Edley

Time is constant;
a continuous
rotation of
seconds, minutes,
and hours
established to
create structure
in the midst
of chaos.

How you utilize your twenty-four hours will determine how effective you will be at life. Prioritizing your day to day, hour to hour routine is necessary for productivity. Allowing God to have authority over your life does not mean He controls you like a puppet. You have to deliver on your end by putting in work and effort. He should certainly take precedence, leading and guiding your decisions but you must be the one to act. Jesus himself had tasks specified to Him which He saw through.

> *I have glorified You on the earth. I have finished the work which You have given Me to do. John 17:4*

He was saying to the Lord: I have heard You. I have exalted You. I have sacrificed. I have done what you have commanded. I have completed the work You set before me to do. I have done what you have required of me. It is finished.

A solid relationship of trust existed between the two, to present the task and see it through. It certainly came with scrutiny, bitterness, sacrifice, and a slew of other things. Things I am sure you yourself have encountered. I assume probably not in the same capacity but this is not to minimize what you have weathered. Can you say to God, right now, I have finished the work You have given me to do? If not, it is okay. At this present time, I cannot say that either. But it is what I aspire to do. To complete the work set before me and glorify Him in the process.

Putting Him first in your life will get the ball rolling.

The very acknowledgement of His presence initiates the basis of a budding relationship. If you do not have a relationship with Him or if it could use some improving, start now. You need to connect to the source. Connecting to Him leads to redemption followed by gratification and fruition.

> *But seek first the kingdom of God and His righteousness, and all these things shall be added to you. Matthew 6:33*

Linking up with Him is a guaranteed victory. Essential, if you want to further your prosperity. However, it is critical to understand the victory is not about you. When He ordained you to be a prophet unto the nations the implication is for you to impact a multitude of people (Jeremiah 1:5). Victory then, is about the many lives you will touch from the relationship you share with God. He has set you apart with a strategic purpose in mind. This purpose far exceeds your imagination. You must actively implement steps to achieve this plan by utilizing your time wisely.

Use your time to be the good for this world. You have to choose to do so. Do not go against what you were made for. Do not make it harder than it needs to be. You can excel at doing well. It actually should come naturally because it is what you were created to do. You were created to do good for the Kingdom.

> *For we are his workmanship, created in*
> *Christ Jesus for good works, which God*
> *prepared beforehand that we should walk*
> *in them. Ephesians 2:10*

Walk in your goodness. You do not have the time to do anything else. If you have the time but are not utilizing it you are delaying the process.

The misconception about time is, we have plenty of it. What is the rush? We will tend to it tomorrow. Or next month. Or next year. But, the reality is, time does not stop for anyone. We become complacent with the belief of putting something off until later. As if the next hour of our lives is guaranteed. This expectation allows us to delay action. We neglect it right now but we will get to it eventually but eventually may not come. If you never want to grow or evolve you will be content holding off on what you desire. Those of us who want to expand our boundaries and think and move outside the box have to make use of the time we are given because we understand the blessing of possessing it and walking in it right now. We crave seeing God's Will on earth as in heaven (Matthew 6:10). We want to be filled and made whole.

> *Blessed are those who hunger and thirst*
> *for righteousness, for they shall be filled.*
> *Matthew 5:6*

Just by hungering after righteousness, thirsting for it,

you are blessed. It does not say you will be blessed it says you already are. *Blessed* is in the past tense. Especially in a world filled with such sin, your desire for righteousness is what will fill you up, continuously, to the point of overflow.

There is purpose in the very breath you breathe. Because you are breathing you are afforded another opportunity to pursue your purpose. Another opportunity to better utilize your time and seek what is good. Whatever you do with your time make sure it is preparing you to advance and prevail. Do not postpone your destiny any longer, drawing out the process even further. The world goes on whether you are involved or not, alive or not. It keeps turning, it keeps revolving and evolving. This constant evolution should convince you of the intricacies of Our Creator. Encouraging you to decide whether to be a part of this progression. It is your time. It is your season to bask in the favor of your Heavenly Father.

> *To everything there is a season, a time to every purpose under the heaven: a time to be born, and a time to die; a time to plant, and a time to pluck what is planted; a time to kill, and a time to heal; a time to break down, and a time to build up; a time to weep, and a time to laugh; a time to mourn, and a time to dance; a time to cast away stones, and a time to gather stones; a time to embrace, and a time to refrain from embracing; a time to gain, and a time*

> *to lose; a time to keep, and a time to throw*
> *away; a time to tear, and a time to sew; a*
> *time to keep silence, and a time to speak; a*
> *time to love, and a time to hate; a time of*
> *war, and a time of peace. Ecclesiastes 3:1-8*

There is a season for things but there is a time for purposes. Seasons only last for a period then they change but there is always a time for each and every purpose. You do not have to go through what you are going through for more than a season. Each season brings change so you should never be stuck for too long. If it did not work for you in this season try a different approach in the next. Consider another idea. Explore other options. Connect with people who have already been there done that and be open to listen to their advice. I am not suggesting you wait for the season to change to change but what better time to shift (especially when things are not in your favor) than when the rhythm of the season shifts with you.

Move when He says move. ***Allow Him to call the shots but you have to be the one to make them.*** He is confident in you because He created you and He knows He never makes mistakes. If He grants you another day He has a purpose for you that has not yet been fulfilled. The very fact you are alive is an implication of your significance. You have a job to do that is made for you to complete. Fortunately, time has been permitted to you in order to fulfill it. You need to wake up eager to make it happen. Whatever it is. Wake up and implement the strategy. God likes to see your determination to complete the task at hand. To be efficient you have to remove distractions and focus on one area at a time. It can be overwhelming chasing after your purpose, staying on the right track, and understanding your role in all of it. Find peace in knowing even in the overwhelming moments God is with you and rooting for you.

We were created with a goal in mind. Unfortunately, most people waste a lot of valuable time tending to unnecessary things. Things hindering them from their journey. Things not conducive to their progression. If there is ever a time to be picky it is always with whatever you allow to take up your time. You can no longer tolerate people who are doing nothing. People who are wasting away in idleness rather than producing. Once we stop procrastinating God will start moving, blessing, equipping, preparing, and building us up.

> *The soul of a lazy man desires, and has nothing; but the soul of the diligent shall be made rich. Proverbs 13:4*

Desire without action is simply a wish. Transforming the desire from a wish to a goal is done so by hard work and dedication. You have to stop putting it off for tomorrow. Or until you have the means. Or until you have a spouse. Or until you are perfect. Or forgiven. You will only know it can be done if you attempt to do it. Put in the time and watch God reward you. It is through your diligence, during your pursuit that He will reward you, sustain you, and promote you.

Pursue your destiny but understand patience is also a part of the process. If it does not happen quickly or in the time you have allotted it does not mean it will not happen. You still have to remain faithful while you pursue. While you work. While you spend countless hours brainstorming, editing, writing, and reading. Patience does not mean do nothing while you wait. Continue moving toward wherever God is leading you, knowing all comes to pass in due time. If it is His plan He will see it through. There are some ideas you may want to shelve, put on the back burner, and focus on His plans. We can get in our own way at times, slowing up the process. We have to step back in order for His plan to take shape. The purpose inside each of us will come to the forefront if we seek it and diligently work to see it through. Begin by trusting in the Lord. It is His plan but your implementation.

Showing Him your faithfulness makes Him want to reward you for your obedience. God will give you more and more abilities as you progress but you must be prepared to utilize your skillset. He is not going to give you more if you have not used what has already been given. Do you remember the account of the men and the talents?

> *He gave five talents to one, two talents to another, one talent to another; all according to their ability. The ones who were given the five and two talents, doubled what they had been given. Yet, the one who was given one talent, hid his talent. The Lord then took the*

> *talent He had given and gave it to the one*
> *who had ten talents. He then rebuked the*
> *servant for doing nothing with what he had*
> *been given. (Matthew 25:14-30).*

Scary, yet we play God in the same way. Hiding our talent (plural for some) due to fear just like the man with one talent. If He was not pleased with the servant for hiding one talent I can assume He would not be pleased with us for doing the same. They were given an opportunity and they were given time to maximize it. After dispersing the talents to the men, he went on a journey.

> *After a long time the lord of those servants*
> *came and settled accounts with them.*
> *Matthew 25:19*

The servants were given *a long time* to make something out of what they had been given. Yet, only two pursued the opportunity (two out of three is pretty good odds). The disadvantage to the one was not only did he lack profitability what he thought he possessed was taken from him and he was condemned. He made excuses which I am sure we all have done in response to our lack of faith and action. He serves as an example for us to take opportunities when they are presented and utilize the gift to fulfill our potential.

Our full potential cannot be pursued if fear is leading our lives. It can only be reached when our desire to achieve our purpose is greater than our fear. It takes full commitment. Our investment will then yield double, triple, quadruple the return. Our level of pursuit is directly related to His level of return. He will give based on what we ask for.

> *Ask, and it will be given to you; seek, and you will find; knock, and it will be opened to you. For every one who asks receives; and he who seeks finds, and to him who knocks it will be opened. Matthew 7:7-8*

God is waiting for you. You are not waiting for God. The time is now to go make progress. It is time to come to the realization that your time on earth is limited which is why every day should serve a purpose. There may be moments of unpredictability but there is intentionality. Speak it, pursue it, and step into it. You know what *it* is but if you are still unsure ask God and He will reveal it. Once He does, go get it. Start your process of progression.

—

Birthdays. I just had one about a week ago on September 28th. 28 on the 28th. My golden birthday. Birthdays are a means of celebrating another year of life. Another opportunity to improve.

We are not all given such an opportunity. I always loved birthdays as a child. Mostly because of the cake and gifts. I do not know a child who does not like sweets and new toys. As I grow older though I am still fond of the cake, but the gifts mean much less to me. I do appreciate them but I appreciate the giver much more. No need for a big celebration with the entire family, I just want the presence of the people who have been present in my life year after year. Not the ones who have been there sporadically or based on convenience but the ones who have rode with me through the ups and downs brought on by the previous year. These are the ones I know can endure. These are the people who will reap the benefits of the blessings.

Those who suffer with me understand the journey. They understand what it took to be where I am today. They celebrate the growth taken place over the year. When I look at the faces of those who have stuck with me another year I am reminded of Gods omnipresence. How He is present year after year of your life whether you have others who stick with you throughout the journey or not. We were not meant to remain tied to everyone and everything. The process is meant to draw on your strengths. It is meant to limit your weaknesses. You go through the process of life in order to sustain evolution so the people who leave you were never meant to stay.

I use to question why a person was no longer present in my life. Whether I was at fault or not but with time I recognized the significance of letting go. Time is limited and I only want to appreciate the ones who appreciate me. I wish no ill-will toward anyone because it is not in my power to condemn them. I will pray for you and move forward. With time, you start to figure out what is most important. You develop an awareness of what really matters. As a child, you should experience the innocence of childhood and understand as you grow it is okay to make mistakes. Experience each stage and age of life. I am currently doing life. Recognizing God's presence in my life has been the most rewarding thing for me. It is different when you form a relationship with Him and not just an idea of who He is. It is critical to maintain this relationship to let the roots take hold.

> *...rooted and built up in Him and established in the faith, as you have been taught, abounding in it with thanksgiving.*
> *Colossians 2:7*

I will keep Him in the forefront because He has kept me. He has established and taught me. Every day I wake up thanking Him. I am blessed and highly favored. I am loved and love in return. The world is full of chaos yet I have peace. All I have been blessed to receive is credited to Him. I can no longer waste His precious time. He has presented me with this present time and I will be obedient to His command.

Every birthday is an advancement. He has afforded me another year of life. I have to do something useful with it. God has called me to be effective. He has called you to be effective. If I can do it, you can do it. I believe it can be done because I know what already has been accomplished. We can achieve great and mighty things; the time is now to attain it. To pursue it. We may not have another year to work toward what we desire. We only have right now. They say why put off for tomorrow what you can do today? It is a valid question. Why not utilize the space you are currently in? Why not maximize every hour of the day? We may not receive another chance to excel which is why the process can no longer be delayed.

All of our progression has led us to this moment of revelation. You should now understand how all the processes of life, all the pain, all the heartache, all the achievements, and accolades are a part of progressing. You cannot progress if you do not go through the process. If you act, you will reach your destination. Take a step in the right direction by following The Leader. By now you should know who The Leader is, God. He will not lead you astray. He will reroute you. Direct you. Instill wisdom into your heart, mind, and soul. You only need to be led. Walking the walk with Him by your side every step of the way. It is He, who will allow you to progress through this process of life.

Printed in the United States
By Bookmasters